Coping With Complexity
How Voters Adapt to Unstable Parties

Dani Marinova

![ecpr PRESS]

First published by the ECPR Press in 2016

Cover: © Ralwel, Dreamstime

The ECPR Press is the publishing imprint of the European Consortium for Political Research (ECPR), a scholarly association, which supports and encourages the training, research and cross-national co-operation of political scientists in institutions throughout Europe and beyond.

ECPR Press
Harbour House
Hythe Quay
Colchester
CO2 8JF
United Kingdom

Typeset by Lapiz Digital Services

Printed and bound by Lightning Source

British Library Cataloguing in Publication Data

A catalogue record for this book is available from the British Library

HARDBACK ISBN: 978-1-785521-51-5
PAPERBACK ISBN: 978-1-785522-60-4
PDF ISBN: 978-1-785521-96-6
EPUB ISBN: 978-1-785521-97-3
KINDLE ISBN: 978-1-785521-98-0

www.ecpr.eu/ecprpress

More in the ECPR Press Monographs series

Please visit http://www.ecpr.eu/ecprpress for information about new publications.

Table of Contents

List of Figures and Tables

Figures

Tables

List of Abbreviations

AN	Alleanza Nazionale
CEE	Central and Eastern Europe
CSES	Comparative Study of Electoral Systems
DC-Nuovo PSI	Christian Democrats – the New Italian Socialist Party
EIP	Electoral Instability in Parties
FI	Forza Italia
LiD	The Left and the Democrats
LN	Lega Nord
LPR	League of Polish Families
NDSV	National Movement Simeon II
PD	Democratic Party
PdL	Il Popolo della Liberta
PiS	Law and Justice
PRC	Communist Refoundation Party
SRP-KPEiR	Self-Defence of the Republic of Poland – National Party of Retirees and Pensioners
UDC	Union of Christian Democrats and Democrats of Centre
VU	People's Union
VU-ID21	People's Union – Flemish Free Democrats
WE	Western Europe

For a full list of political party titles and abbreviations, please see Appendix: Party Names

Acknowledgements

I came of age during the 2001 parliamentary election in Bulgaria. It was an exciting and unpredictable campaign that brought about the election of Bulgaria's former king into the nation's highest political office. The election season was marked by a feeling of patriotism surely related to the return of the monarch as well as by a palpable feeling of change. Indeed the election had shaken up a party system hitherto dominated by two parties. The political platform of the king materialized just months before the election and was possibly the trigger of a series of splinters and coalitions among existing parties. The reconfiguration of the party system slipped under my radar at the time. Five years on, as I pursued my doctoral studies at Indiana University – Bloomington, I wondered if and how such instability affected voters' decision-making at the polls. This book offers answers to this question.

As this book came into being, I received support and encouragement from a number of individuals. My Ph.D. adviser Timothy Hellwig has been a great mentor, colleague and friend. His dedication to my work is deeply appreciated. I thank the members of my dissertation committee, Jack Bielasiak, Edward Carmines and John Kruschke, for their guidance and feedback. I thank Robert Rohrschneider for his mentorship during the first years of my Ph.D. and for awakening in me an interest in political behaviour. The manuscript has improved thanks to the thoughtful comments of Eva Anduiza, Ian Anson, Nicholas D'Amico, Ruth Dassonneville, Cees van der Eijk, Mark Franklin, Carolina Galais, Bradley Gomez, Kenneth Janda, Ender Duygu Kavas, Jordi Muñoz, Guillem Rico, Peter Söderlund and several anonymous reviewers.[1] My editor Alexandra Segerberg and the reviewers at the ECPR Press offered many helpful suggestions as I revised the manuscript.

I am grateful to acknowledge a grant from the National Science Foundation that funded the data collection for this project (Doctoral Dissertation Improvement Grant in Political Science, SES-1065761). Over the years, I have benefited from a number of additional grants that have helped support my research. I gratefully acknowledge a Mellon Endowment grant from the Russian and East European Institute, a Women in Science Program grant from the Office of Women's Affairs and a research grant from the European Union Centre of Excellence, all at Indiana University. The final stages of this project were financed by a Juan de la Cierva grant from the Spanish Ministry of Science and Education. I am indebted to the

---

1. Two of the chapters in this book were published previously as journal articles. A section of Chapter 4 was published in 2015 as "A New Approach to Estimating Electoral Instability in Parties" in *Political Science Research and Methods* (Vol. 3, Issue 2, pp. 265–280). A more elaborate version of Chapter 5 was published in 2016 as "Political Knowledge in Complex Information Environments" in *Acta Politica* (Vol 51, Issue 2, pp. 194–213). I thank the anonymous reviewers of both journals for their suggestions on improving the manuscript.

Democracy, Elections and Citizenship Research Group at Universitat Autònoma de Barcelona for offering me an academic home during the 2011–2012 academic year as I completed my dissertation. Ian Anson and Nicholas D'Amico helped me collect data on party instability, and I thank them for their valuable research assistance.

I would be remiss if I did not acknowledge support from my family and friends. Without the partnership of my husband Ignasi Lucas, I would struggle to combine family life with an academic career. His support has been instrumental in completing this manuscript. I am deeply grateful to Luciana Pastori and Theodora Bagiati who cared for our son and who gave me the peace of mind I needed to dedicate myself to research. The friendship of Ender Duygu Kavas, Ivana Tuzharova, Le Anh Long and Jessie Wang has meant a lot to me over the years. I dedicate the book to Betty Dorris and Joe Graves whose openheartedness inspires me to this day.

Bellaterra, June 2016

Chapter One

Coping with Complexity: Introduction to the Research Problem

Imagine you were a voter in Greece's election in January of 2015. The election was historic; it brought about the first radical-left government in Europe's post-war history. It was also highly dynamic. The party system was undergoing profound transformation over the previous electoral cycles in 2012 and into 2015. Consider that for decades Greece was essentially a two-party system, with PASOK and New Democracy sharing roughly 80 per cent of the popular vote. Their share was reduced to 40 per cent in 2012 and to just 30 per cent in 2015. Since then, a dozen or so parties have been created, most of them splinters from PASOK or New Democracy (e.g., Pact for a New Greece (PASOK splinter), Union for the Homeland and the People (ND splinter) and Plan B (SYRIZA splinter)). Political personalities, like TV presenter Stavros Theodorakis, also launched new parties that proved to be electorally successful despite their vague policy stances. Some of these parties went on to merge or form joint lists with other newcomers (e.g., the newly formed splinter Reformers for Democracy and Development and Theodorakis' The River). The 2012 and 2015 elections saw some of the most colourful, and most fragmented, distribution of parliamentary seats in modern Greek history.

This book is not concerned so much with the success of new and transformed parties as it is with the electoral complexity that party changes generate for voters. Consider that a Greek voter in 2015 could not rely on his or her stored knowledge or past experiences with political parties in the same way that a Greek voter could in the 2004 or 2007 parliamentary elections. In the latter, the main contenders were long-standing parties with whose policies and performance records voters were closely familiar. In 2015 in contrast, a voter would need to seek out information on the largely unknown new and transformed party organisations, including their ideology, policy positions and competences. How do voters cope with the electoral complexity triggered by instability in party organisations? And what are the implications for democratic representation in elections?

This book is about how voters make decisions. It looks particularly at how voters seek out information, apply decision-making heuristics and elect viable policy makers. I offer a novel answer to these old questions by taking into account the quality and the diffusion of information in elections. I argue that political parties are central to structuring and communicating electoral information. Parties organise messy, 'raw' information about ideology, policy goals and competences into a coherent set of electoral alternatives. Thanks to the informational cues that parties offer, voters are able to access information at a low cognitive cost and to choose readily viable policy makers. When parties undergo abrupt organisational changes between elections – e.g., when they fuse, split, or take part in or abandon party joint lists – they profoundly alter the organisation and supply of electoral information. The electoral alternatives on the ballot are no longer fixed or presented as such to the voter but need to be actively sought out and cognitively constructed instead. Regular citizens need to do more of the work in acquiring, attributing and processing electoral information. I argue that this has important consequences for electoral behaviour. Namely, voters cope with the complexity of such electoral races by acquiring relatively little information in elections and by using an alternative set of low-information heuristics to discern and decide between parties.

Insights on the facilitating role of parties in voter decision-making allow me to shift attention to the principal actors who provide voters with cues in elections—political parties—and to reexamine the theories predominantly used to understand electoral behaviour from this new perspective. Extant explanations of the differences in information seeking and electoral decision-making have predominantly focused on voters' characteristics (e.g., level of education) and institutional setups (e.g., electoral institutions). Important as they are, these factors nonetheless neglect that voters rely on political parties to simplify public choices effectively. Party instability has received considerable academic attention in the study of electoral and party systems; yet its effects on the electoral information environment and on voters' decision-making have thus far not been well understood. A closer look at the impact of party instability on the vote promises to advance our extant knowledge of voter behaviour and to qualify quintessential theories of vote choice, including proximity voting (Downs 1957), direction-intensity appeals (Rabinowitz and Macdonald 1989), economic voting (Powell and Whitten 1993), the use of informational heuristics (Tversky and Kahneman 1974) and dual-processing theories (Petty and Cacioppo 1986). The empirical analyses rely on survey, party and national data from a large set of European elections, from both advanced industrialised and young democracies. The rich and nuanced findings illustrate that political parties hold a key to understanding electoral behaviour and representation in modern democracy.

Parties and party instability in representative democracy

Change in political parties is commonplace in modern democracies. Nearly five decades ago Carl Friedrich observed (1968):

> Party development is more highly dynamic than any other sphere of political life; there is no final rest, no ultimate pattern... Rather, there is constant change in one direction or another, with never a return to that starting point (p. 452).

Party instability – or the organisational changes parties undergo between electoral cycles – is a phenomenon which is just as relevant in the study of electoral politics today as it was in 1968 (Birch 2001; Mair 1997; Mair *et al.* 2004; Powell and Tucker 2014; Sikk 2005; 2012).[1] What is more, changes in party organisations are frequent in old and new democracies alike. Instability has become common in the consolidated party systems of West Europe. It marks a process of electoral dealignment that initiated in the 1970s and 1980s (Maguire 1983; Mair *et al.* 2004). Party instability is also a defining feature of the new party systems in Central and Eastern Europe (Bielasiak 2002; Sikk 2005; Tavits 2008a). It has been critical to understanding politics in the region and has received ample academic attention.

As prevalent as party instability is across democracies, its implications for electoral decision-making are not well understood. At least two recent studies have gestured towards the importance of party organisations in explaining vote choice and electoral representation but none has pursued these questions head-on (Ezrow *et al.* 2014; Rohrschneider and Whitefield 2012). More generally, the facilitating role of political parties in voter information seeking and decision-making has been subject to little empirical scrutiny. Paul Sniderman and colleagues have made convincing arguments for parties' crucial roles in structuring and communicating electoral information to voters (Brady and Sniderman 1985; Jackman and Sniderman 2002; Sniderman 2000). However, empirical research in electoral behaviour and political psychology has not followed up on Sniderman's theoretical propositions. Instead, it has relied on the unstated assumption that the electoral alternatives on the ballot are equally well defined and continuous over electoral cycles and that parties are equally effective in simplifying and transmitting information across elections. In considering the role of party instability in electoral decision-making, this book seeks to shed light on how decision-making processes unfold in less well-structured electoral spaces.

More fundamentally, this work is an effort to assess the extent to which citizens can make sense of the order of politics and elect parties that represent their interests (cf. Roberts 2009). Taking a step back to broader debates on electoral representation and democracy, we can identify a widespread consensus that free, competitive elections, more than any other feature of the modern nation-state, signal the presence of a democratic political system (Powell 2000, p.4).[2] Elections are 'the instruments of democracy' so long as they successfully fulfill two functions: citizens elect political parties that will represent them in policymaking; and voters hold incumbents accountable for their performance in office (Lippman 1925; Mill 1958; Powell 2000; Tocqueville 1945). As many scholars have argued elsewhere, the extant literature takes us only so far in understanding why democratic elections link citizens to their representatives in some countries and election years yet do not

---

1. The ECPR announced a workshop titled "Rethinking Intra-Party Cohesion in Time of Party Transformation" for its 2017 Joint Sessions.

2. 'We would be reluctant to consider any system a representative government unless it held regular elections which were "genuine" or "free"' (Pitkin 1967, pp.234–235).

successfully do so in others (Nadeau *et al.* 2000; Powell 2004).[3] This book places political parties at the centre of electoral representation and accountability as they are critical to both processes. Parties provide the informational cues without which the masses would struggle to discern the ideology, policy goals and competences of competing actors. And without this information, voters are likely to struggle in making the reasoned decisions which form the foundations of a working representative democracy. In considering the role of parties and party instability in voters' electoral calculus, this book promises to shed new light on the workings and pitfalls of modern democracy.

What is new

A rich literature on electoral behaviour and political psychology informs our understanding of how voters make choices. One of the major breakthroughs in the behavioural social sciences is the advent of cognitive heuristics, for which Daniel Kahneman and Amos Tversky received the Nobel Prize in Economics in 2002.[4] Heuristics were thought to have resolved one of the greatest puzzles in political behaviour – namely, how citizens, generally held to be uninformed and apathetic about public affairs, come to make reasonably good electoral decisions (Lupia and McCubbins 1998; Popkin 1991; Sniderman, Glazer, and Griffin 1990). Though not without their critics (e.g., Bartels 1996), efficient judgmental shortcuts have been generally appreciated for aiding voters make decisions (for a recent review, see Carmines and D'Amico 2015). This book joins several other works in questioning the focus in studying the use of heuristics in electoral decision-making (Brady and Sniderman 1985; Jackman and Sniderman 2002; Sniderman 2000). Much of the scholarly research has narrowed in on citizens' cognitive resources in facilitating their ability to use heuristics. In contrast to earlier research, this book takes a step back to examine the role of voters' information environments in facilitating the use of decision-making shortcuts. In particular, it considers how parties structure political conflict into a simplified set of alternatives and communicate these alternatives to voters. Investigating the role of party instability in voters' information environments helps assess parties' facilitating roles in voter decision-making and re-examine the importance of citizens' cognitive abilities in heuristics use. This book thus integrates parties and party systems into the study of heuristics and into theories of vote choice more broadly.

Furthermore, the book speaks to an empirical puzzle which has motivated one of the largest subfields in political behaviour – why electoral accountability

---

3. Nadeau *et al.* (2002) give examples of unexplained differences in levels of political accountability across time and space while Powell (2004) points out that macro-institutional theories of political representation leave out considerable unexplained variation in developing democracies.

4. Redlawsk and Lau (2013, p. 137) define heuristics as 'problem-solving strategies (often employed automatically or unconsciously), which serve to keep the information processing demands of the task within bounds' (original quotes omitted).

is fulfilled only in some elections (Anderson and Hecht 2012; Paldam 1991; Powell and Whitten 1993; Whitten and Palmer 1999).[5] Research in economic voting has offered answers ranging from citizens' demonstrated tendency to form skewed perceptions of systemic outputs and government performance (Nadeau *et al.* 2000; Nadeau *et al.* 1999; Sanders and Gavin 2004) to their displayed difficulty gaging which political actors should be held responsible for systemic outputs under complex institutional setups (Powell and Whitten 1993; Whitten and Palmer 1999). Such accounts of the voting calculus focus overly on structural explanations (e.g., institutions) that remain relatively stable over the medium and long terms. As a result, extant theories struggle to account for unexplained inter-election variation in the presence and strength of electoral accountability. Furthermore, institutions are only a secondary force in shaping electoral politics because politicians and voters learn – and learn to manipulate – the rules of the game over time (Kitschelt, Mansfeldova, *et al.* 1999, p.12). The actions of political actors have thus far not taken front stage in understanding variation in economic voting across elections.

Party instability is a game-changer when it comes to theories of economic voting. In contrast to the extant literature, I argue that the economic vote is not suited to all elections. Conventional wisdom has it that the economic voter casts a ballot either for or against the incumbent based on one simple piece of information – the state of the economy. I argue that this is an overly simplistic understanding of the economic vote. Consider that effective economic voting requires not only information about the state of the economy but also voters' judgments on whether or not such information is a good predictor of *future* governing capacity and performance. In regard to the latter, changes in parties are essential to assessing governing capacity and may override strict economic retrospections. As a result, strict retrospective voting on economic considerations may not necessarily be an optimal voting strategy for altered parties. I argue that the stability of the electoral alternatives conditions the viability of economic retrospections as a decision-making rule. Party instability thus qualifies the universal desirability of economic voting across elections.

By integrating political parties into electoral decision-making, this book takes into account the active role of party organisations in the processes of electoral representation and thus equips parties with the *agency* to influence voter choice. Parties' behaviour is essential to a functioning representative democracy. Elster *et al.* (1998) write, 'The structure and the interaction of political parties are the

---

5. Whitten and Palmer (1999) report considerable variation in inter-election accountability (as do Lewis-Beck 1988 and Paldam 1991). However, static institutional theories do not make clear why, for example, voters have been able to sanction parties for poor performance in Denmark since 1973 but not before or why accountability works only in some elections in Germany (Anderson 1995; Nadeau *et al.* 2002; Rattinger and Kramer 1998). The limitations of present theories are also reflected in the 'striking failures of large-district PR rules to generate proportional outcomes in a number of new democracies of Eastern Europe,' despite what low-threshold PR rules would predict (Powell 2004, p.279).

most significant variables which contribute to the consolidation or failure of the political systems of democratic politics' (pp.110–111). Despite the widely recognised import of parties to the functioning of electoral democracy, little has been done to integrate the rich and intricate world of party organisations in theories of voter behaviour. My account of parties as potentially divisive organisations moves away from static models of voter behaviour. In the latter, parties are merely the recipients of voters' evaluations and responsibility attributions under fixed institutional settings and are not equipped with the agency to influence voters' decision-making in turn. This book thus conceives of elections in fairly realistic terms – as dynamic, give-and-take processes between voters and parties. Considering the effects of party change on how voters decide begins to close an important gap in the interaction between political parties and voters. To my knowledge, this is the first study to examine systematically the linkage between the agency of political parties to change their organisational structure and the ability of citizens to make good electoral decisions.

Finally, this book has much to say about the internal processes of political parties and party systems. Recent scholarship has pointed out problems in the conceptualisation and measurement of party change (Birch 2001; Mair 1997; Powell and Tucker 2013; Tavits 2008). These problems pose challenges for empirical research and theory development in the subfields of party and electoral systems and in the broader comparative literature. The complexity of party dynamics usually means that they are studied qualitatively and are limited to a handful of cases (e.g., Dix 1992; Kreuzer and Pettai 2003; Protsyk and Wilson 2003; Sikk 2012; Shabad and Slomczynski 2004). My research makes an empirical contribution in producing a large, comparative data set on party instability in a diverse set of political systems. Unlike existing approximations of the prevalence of party instability in elections, these data minimise measurement error and can facilitate quantitative inquiries of parties, party systems and their interaction with voting behaviour, well beyond this book.

Empirical approach

Pedersen (1979) famously defined party system instability as changes in the patterns of interaction and competition between both parties and the electorate (p.4). Despite his broad and oft-cited definition, the study of party system change has focused primarily on changes originating from shifts in *voter* preferences, to the neglect of change originating from parties.[6] Currently used measures of party system change either focus on the voter side of the equation or do not do enough to separate changes originating from parties and those

---

6. This imbalance is easily demonstrated by the prevalent use of the Pedersen index of electoral volatility (Bartolini and Mair 1990; Coppedge 1998; Ersson and Lane 1998; Korasteleva 2000; Lane 2008; Mainwaring 1998; Mainwaring and Zoco 2007; Meleshevich 2007; Pedersen 1979; Robbins and Hunter 2012; Tóka 1997).

originating from voters.[7] As a result extant measures obfuscate the nature of instability in party systems. The endogeneity between parties and voters in extant indices of party system change render them inadequate for the study of voter response to party change.

I develop a measure of party system instability that can be traced to changes in political parties rather than voter preferences. To do so, I collect data on a wide range of indicators of party change: the emergence of new parties, the disbanding of existing parties, party mergers, splinter parties, and party entry into and exit from joint lists. From these detailed, qualitative data, I compose an aggregate, standardised index of party change to facilitate the empirical examination of how voters respond to party instability. By focusing on changes and continuities in party organisations, the new measure compliments Pedersen's index of electoral volatility and helps limit the conflation of different sources of party system instability. The data stand apart from existing indicators of electoral volatility in that they estimate party system instability independently of election results and mass preferences and reduce endogeneity concerns in the study of party maneuvering and voter choice.

To understand the interaction between political parties and voters, I complement this original data set with individual, survey data from the Comparative Study of Electoral Systems (CSES). The CSES offers some of the best quality elections data in the field. A common module of questions is administered either just before or directly after an election, thus making the CSES ideal for the study of electoral behaviour. The CSES offers a random sample of elections and voters by using a two-stage sampling procedure. It first draws a sample of elections and then a sample of voters nested in these elections. In addition to individual survey responses, the CSES provides data on parties and electoral institutions which are critical control variables in the empirical models in Chapters Four, Five and Six. These reasons rendered the CSES the most appropriate data base of elections for testing the theoretical predictions of this study.

The emphasis on understanding how distinct political environments condition voting behaviour naturally gives the project a comparative flavour. To test the implications of the theoretical framework developed in Chapter Two, I use a sample of elections from both mature and young European democracies in the past twenty-five years. This sample includes the advanced industrialised democracies of Western Europe and the ten continuously democratic post-socialist countries. I contend that it is meaningful to compare these two sets of democracies. Previous research indicates that theories of political representation and accountability derived from the experiences of Western Europe are also relevant to understanding electoral politics in the young democracies of post-communist Europe. Namely, parties in the latter have been shown to be programmatically organised and ideologically coherent (Kitschelt, Mansfeldova, *et al.* 1999; Rohrschneider and

---

7. A number of recent studies treat electoral volatility as akin to instability in parties and party systems (e.g., Bielasiak 1997; 2002; Evans 2002; Maguire 1983; Mainwaring and Zoco 2007; Meleshevich 2007; Taagepera and Grofman 2003).

Whitefield 2009; Whitefield and Rohrschneider 2009) while voters have been shown to hold ideologically-structured and stable political preferences (Kitschelt, Lange, *et al.* 1999; Tworzecki 2002). Rates of ideological voting in the region are comparable to those in established democracies, and in some post-socialist elections, very high electoral volatility coexists with high rates of ideological voting (Mainwaring and Torcal 2006). Furthermore, there is ample evidence that economic performance shapes vote choice in post-communist democracies, just as it does in mature democracies (Roberts 2008). Given this evidence, it is meaningful to examine the extent to which instability in parties conditions voter behaviour and electoral representation across new and mature democratic systems.[8]

Plan of the book

This contribution seeks to understand the linkages between the organisation of electoral spaces and the processes of voter decision-making. In Chapter Two, I construct the theoretical framework of the party-voter nexus. Like many scholars before me, I conceive of elections as information environments that can limit the amount and the clarity of information voters have at their disposal. I demonstrate that political parties are the principal actors who structure and supply information in elections. In doing so, parties condition the quality and diffusion of information to voters. Once we appreciate how parties facilitate information to voters, we can chart preliminary expectations of the potential effects of party instability on the vote. The theoretical framework predicts that voters will cope, consecutively, through a series of passive and active adaptation strategies. Facing higher costs to information, voters will remain passively uninformed rather than actively seek to overcome information barriers. Left with less information at their disposal about new and transformed parties, voters will then actively seek coping mechanisms.

Using dual-processing theories as a starting point, I develop expectations of how voters adapt to unstable parties. I consider a series of decision-making strategies that have been shown to work in low-information environments. Among others, I consider voters' propensity to decide based on the intensity of party appeals (rather than exact policy positions), on their gut feelings towards party leaders and on evaluations of the economy. Each of these decision-making strategies has been lauded for requiring little effort and information on the part of voters and therefore fits the bill of the type of decision-making heuristic voters need in complex elections. Dual-processing theory in cognitive psychology offers an important preliminary insight as to how voters will cope with the electoral complexity generated by party instability, but it has thus far not considered the

---

8.   While the heterogeneous democratic experiences of these polities allow me to test the theoretical expectations over a diverse set of elections, they also raise endogeneity concerns. Recent research finds 'volatile' parties, not 'stable' voters, to be the moving force in post-socialist party systems (Rose and Munro 2009; Tavits 2008), suggesting that the causality arrow, from parties to voters, is pointed in the right direction.

specific effects of fluid electoral alternatives. I argue that changing electoral alternatives challenge the logic of some low-information heuristics and can trigger their own unique set of coping mechanisms (what I label 'the party instability heuristic') to cope with uncertainty. Chapter Two testifies to the importance of considering the unique characteristics of low-information elections and their specific impacts on the cognitive processing of information.

Before I test the viability of each of these low-information voting strategies, I identify an adequate indicator of party instability. Chapter Three reviews existing indicators of party system change, their limitations and recent modifications and charts new paths for understanding and measuring party change. I consider the unit of analysis in conceptualising and measuring party change as well as the nature of party change and its relationship with party system change. I proceed to describe the detailed, qualitative data that I have collected from ten post-socialist and seventeen advanced industrialised European democracies, 1987–2011. I then propose an index of party change based on the emergence of new parties, the disbanding of existing parties, party mergers, splinter parties and party entry into and exit from joint lists. I test the external validity of the index by comparing party instability to electoral volatility. The latter indicator picks up on a set of different phenomena across party systems, suggesting that its use may be misleading in comparative research. The chapter concludes with a descriptive analysis of party instability over time and across European elections.

Chapters Four, Five and Six contain the core empirical research on information seeking and decision-making under unstable parties. Using the data on party instability described in Chapter Three, I test the empirical implications of the theory developed in Chapter Two. The first of the empirical chapters examines information seeking while the latter two investigate decision-making mechanisms. Chapter Four tackles the following question: does party instability stymie the acquisition of electoral information about parties? That is, can elections characterised by high party instability be characterised as 'low-information' environments? The empirical analyses answer in the affirmative. Due to the higher demands placed on their attention and cognition by unstable parties, voters were generally less capable of taking party cues as parties erratically transform. This finding has several nuances. First, I find that the relationship is conditional on voters' educational backgrounds. As overall instability increases, the positive effect of education on political knowledge diminishes, suggesting that even the well-educated have difficulty coping with electoral complexity as parties change. Second, the impact of instability was not uniform across the type of changes parties underwent. While voters tended to know less about new parties, they were more knowledgeable about newly formed mergers and joint lists. Overall, the findings suggest that party instability renders elections as low-information environments.

Equipped with little policy information to decide on, how do voters adapt their decision-making to unstable parties? In Chapter Five, I compare the heuristics voters use for stable and unstable parties, respectively. The empirical analyses suggest that voters are generally less likely to decide based on unstable parties' exact positions in policy space and more likely to decide on direction and intensity appeals as compared to stable parties. As a result, in a fluid election like Greece's in 2015, voters are considerably more likely to elect parties with extreme ideological positions. I also find support for the use of a party instability heuristic; in an effort to minimise risk and uncertainty, voters opt for the familiar, stable parties on the ballot and to shy away from newcomers. Finally, the results also indicate a greater role for candidate appeals under unstable parties. New parties are usually not as embedded in the social and political cleavages as long-standing parties (Grofman *et al.* 2000; Ramonaitė 2007). As a result they more often appeal to voters on salient political personalities rather than policy positions.[9] Together the results from Chapter Five suggest that voters facing unstable political parties rely systematically on a unique set of decision-making rules that aid them in adapting to the lower levels of policy information.

Chapter Six puts another low-information strategy of voting – the economic vote – to empirical testing. Given that economic voting is generally held to be less informationally or cognitively demanding (Key 1966; Fiorina 1981; Basinger and Lavine 2005), are voters more likely to simplify the voting calculus and to rely on retrospective economic considerations? The theoretical discussion and empirical results I offer in Chapter Six answer in the negative. I argue that party instability comes head-to-head with the logic of economic voting and makes it less rational on the part of voters to rely on strict economic retrospections when casting a ballot for the incumbent. Party instability interrupts the continuity of the organisation and adds considerable uncertainty about the extent to which past performance is a good predictor of parties' future governing capacity. I conduct two sets of analyses to probe these expectations: (1) at the micro level, I examine how retrospective evaluations of government performance predict vote choice under varying degrees of party instability; (2) at the macro level, I test the extent to which economic performance predicts the electoral fortune of the incumbent when parties are unstable. Both sets of analyses suggest that voters rely on economic retrospections more sparingly as parties transform. Much in contrast to previous research, this book does not ring the alarm bell on weak economic voting. Where party instability is high, economic retrospections alone would not offer voters a good sense of parties' governing capacities after the election. As a result, weaker economic voting is cause for celebrating reasoned vote choice rather than concern.

The final chapter presents an overview of the key arguments and empirical results as well as a discussion of their implications for theories of political behaviour. The book offers only an initial glimpse at how voters decide under unstable parties. The analyses nonetheless uncover fascinating variation that ought to prompt interest in and further research on the topic. Chapters Five and Six document a set of unique and systematic mechanisms of coping with electoral complexity. When the electoral ground under voters shifts, they use different sets of heuristics as they decide between stable and unstable parties. The results hint

---

9. In Greece's 2015 election, Theodorakis' party The River is a case in point. With a prominent TV personality as its leader, the party ran on only a vague policy platform.

at the possibility that our understanding of heuristics and their use in electoral behaviour is only partial. Extant theory has been informed by electoral contexts that are stable rather than erratic and where parties deliver a coherently structured set of electoral alternatives. In less well-structured electoral spaces, however, voters decide between parties by adapting a series of unique heuristics suited for low-information environments. Erratic electoral spaces may thus be ripe new ground for reexamining standard theories of political behaviour and for generating a new set of understandings as to how voters adapt to more hostile electoral environments.

Chapter Two

Voting in Complex Information Environments: A Theoretical Framework

This book traces the consequences of instability in party organisations for citizens' capacity to elect parties that represent their interests in policy making. It is an attempt to understand how citizens, who are generally held to be uninformed and apathetic about public affairs, come to make good electoral choices. The answer has long been that voters make use of efficient judgmental shortcuts, or heuristics, by relying on cues from parties (Downs 1957; Lupia and McCubbins 1998; Popkin 1991; Sniderman, Glazer, and Griffin 1990). In investigating this process, the focus has been placed on the *voters* who rely on party cues rather than on the *parties* who supply them. Scholars have convincingly shown that citizens' cognitive abilities and motivation play a major role in their capacity to use heuristics (Lau 2003; Lau and Redlawsk 2001; Rahn 1993). What has received much less attention is the quality and coherence of the electoral information parties provide. Such information is the foundation on which voters use judgmental shortcuts and make reasoned decisions.

This chapter constructs the theoretical architecture against which the voter-party nexus is explored in the remainder of the book. The foundational base of my argument is that we can conceive of elections as information environments that readily supply, or limit, the amount and the clarity of information voters receive about electoral politics and thereby the role such information plays in their electoral decision-making. Once we do so, the focus of inquiry shifts from the static characteristics of voters and institutions to *the quality and the diffusion of electoral information*. A central pillar of my argument is that political parties are of principal interest as we try to understand the quality of the informational environment in which voters find themselves. Parties have a critical role in structuring political conflict into a simplified set of electoral alternatives and communicating these alternatives at election time (c.f. Brady and Sniderman 1985; Jackman and Sniderman 2002; Sniderman 2000). The accessibility of information at a low cost to voters – and by extension, voters' ability to make informed decisions – depends on parties' fulfilling their informational roles in elections.

Once we appreciate how parties structure voters' information environments, we can begin to build expectations about the potential effect of party instability on voter choice. I argue that the effect is two-fold. First, instability in parties raises the cost of acquiring information to voters; as a result voters will be less knowledgeable about the electoral alternatives before them. I characterise this first effect as *passive* on the part of voters – given the lower quality of information and its poorer communication, voters *are left uninformed* about parties' policy positions. I characterise the second effect of party instability as voters' *active response* to having limited information. Voters will actively *seek coping mechanisms* within contexts of frequent party instability. When voters have more limited information to decide on, they will resort to alternative decision-making strategies that can be adapted to low-information environments. Specifically, I consider voters' propensity to decide based on the intensity of party appeals (rather than exact policy positions), on gut feelings towards party leaders and on evaluations of economic performance. Each of these decision-making strategies has been lauded for requiring little effort and information on the part of voters and therefore fits the bill of the type of decision-making heuristic voters would need in complex elections.

The chapter is structured as follows. Having repositioned our understanding of elections as information environments, I continue on to delimit extant knowledge of the factors which facilitate voter decision-making. I do so through the lens of theories of voter choice in modern democracies which are the focus of the empirical investigation in Chapters Four–Six. My recap of the literature is that existing explanations rest on the individual characteristics of voters or the institutional features of the political system. I identify the absence of political parties as actors who can potentially shape electoral decision-making by either facilitating or stymieing electoral information. In the sections that follow, I outline how political parties are generally thought to structure and communicate information in elections. Against this background, I proceed to consider the potential consequences of instability in political parties for voters' information seeking and their electoral calculus as well as for political representation more broadly.

Elections as information environments: Lessons and limitations

We can conceptualise of elections as environments which readily facilitate, or impede, electoral information to voters.[1] This approach is fruitful in that it allows us to examine simultaneously a variety of factors that play a role in voters' acquisition and processing of information (Luskin 1990). When it comes to individual factors, each voter possesses a unique combination of inherent capacity and motivation to learn and process information about politics. As a result of differences in cognitive and motivational resources, voters embedded in the same election will acquire different levels of information to integrate in their electoral decision-making and will make decisions that vary in their quality (c.f. Huckfeldt and Sprague 1995; Kuklinski *et al.* 2001; Law and Redlawsk 2001; 2006; Lupia and McCubbins 1998; Rahn *et al.* 1994; Sniderman *et al.* 1990). Conceiving of elections as environments that produce and diffuse information allows us to explore further the features of the context in which elections take place. Each election provides a unique set of opportunities – for example, in the competitiveness of the electoral race – to

---

1.   Information environments are defined as systematic characteristics of the political system, exogenous to voters' preferences (Huckfeldt and Sprague 1995; Lupia and McCubbins 1998; Sniderman *et al.* 1990).

learn about party platforms. Different contexts vary in the amount and quality of information they supply to citizens and thus result in further discrepancies in how individuals make decisions. Individual and contextual factors, and their implications for information seeking and reasoned decision-making, are examined in turn.

First, let us briefly review the individual attributes which facilitate the acquisition of political information. Individual differences in socioeconomic resources are among the strongest predictors of information-seeking as socioeconomic resources have a direct impact on the cost of acquiring new information (Althaus 2003; Alvarez and Brehm 2002; Bennet 1989; Delli Carpini and Keeter 1996; Luskin 1990). Individuals of low socioeconomic resources experience higher barriers to learning about politics than do individuals of high socioeconomic status, particularly the well-educated (Converse 1964; Luskin 1987; Zaller 1992). Other socio-demographics also play a role, including gender, but the political sophistication conferred by socioeconomic status and education is the primary demarcating line for individuals' abilities to learn about politics (Fraile 2014). In addition, individuals differ in how driven they are to learn about politics (Curran *et al.* 2009). Here, political interest is the strongest predictor of motivation to learn, but political interest is fundamentally shaped by, and thus overlaps with, the effects of demographic characteristics. Hence, voters' socioeconomic status, and particularly education, affects the resources and motivation at their disposal to learn about politics.

These individual differences in information seeking have repercussions for the quality of decisions voters make at the ballot box. Differences in resources and motivation to keep politically informed have a direct impact on citizens' resources to *process* information (Fiske *et al.* 1983; McGraw and Pinney 1990; Zaller 1992). Research in cognitive psychology has long demonstrated that motivation and the availability of information drive the effort citizens exert in making decisions (Chaiken 1980; Maheswaran and Chaiken 1991). The pure supply of information is not enough for good decisions to take place. The usefulness of the information supplied in elections depends on voter ability to relate new information (e.g., that a new party is left of centre) to their existing knowledge structures (e.g., the left-right ideological spectrum and their own ideology) (Conover and Feldman 1989). Political sophistication – the information voters hold as well as their ability to process it correctly – is central to understanding the quality of electoral decisions (Lau and Redlawsk 2001; 2006).

To illustrate, let us take the following two examples: programmatic voting and economic voting. In electoral decision-making, voting based on programmatic appeals and retrospective evaluations is held to constitute good decision-making (e.g., Lau and Redlawsk 2001; Powell and Whitten 1993). Voting on programmatic grounds allows voters to elect parties that will most closely represent their policy preferences while voting on retrospective evaluations of the incumbent will allow decision-makers to hold incumbents accountable for their past performance in office; voter-party policy congruence and electoral accountability for past performance are in turn held as the central pillars of representative democracy.

Both programmatic and retrospective voting depend on some amount of information and information-processing. When it comes to programmatic voting, voters will first need sufficient information to place parties on an ideological continuum and will then need the cognitive resources to link their own political beliefs to those of parties. When it comes to sanctioning incumbents for their performance in office, voters should first be able to distinguish between parties that were in government and those that were not and should then be able to attribute policy performance to political incumbents rather than exogenous conditions beyond the government's control. Variation in political sophistication has been shown to make an empirical difference in voters' propensity to elect competent and ideologically similar policy makers; voting varies systematically with political sophistication as sophisticates cast ideologically consistent votes, attribute responsibility to less obvious targets and divide responsibility fairly among multiple actors (Gomez and Wilson 2006; Koch, 1998; Luskin, 1987; Palfrey and Poole 1987; Pattie and Johnston 2001; Rudolph 2003; Sniderman, Brody, and Tetlock, 1993; Zaller, 1992).

In addition to the individual characteristics of voters, the study of voter behaviour has shifted in recent decades to consider the effects of *contextual* factors on the supply of political information. The shift is justified by the large variation in information levels observed among voters embedded in different elections (Curran *et al.* 2009; Fraile 2014). That is, in addition to differences between individuals in the same election, scholars have also observed systematic between-election differences in information seeking and reasoned decision-making. To understand contextual sources of variation in the supply of information, a number of scholars have placed at the centre of inquiry cross-national differences in electoral institutions. Central to their analyses are those institutions whose features have predictable effects on information seeking and acquisition: e.g., proportional representation systems with coalition governments and a large number of parties, and bicameral legislatures, among others (Berggren 2000; Fraile 2014; Gordon and Segura 1997; Grönlund and Milner 2006). It has been shown, for example, that when institutions are rather complex, as is the case of bicameral legislative systems and coalition governments, the level of information held by citizens is on average lower than in unicameral legislatures and single-party governments. In multi-party systems, where parties try to differentiate themselves from competitors by sending clear cues to voters, electoral competition offers voters better opportunities to acquire information than it does voters in two-party systems. Each country's unique set of institutions drive, on one hand, a convergence in information-seeking among individuals within the same context and, on the other hand, a predictable divergence in levels of political knowledge between countries as well as between elections within the same country.

Informational differences between contexts carry implications for the quality of electoral decision-making. Depending on the context they are in, voters are supplied with more, or less, electoral information which in turn facilitates, or stymies, its use in electoral decision-making. One well-studied election-level variable that facilitates programmatic voting is the competitiveness of the electoral race (Basinger and Lavine 2005; Gronke 2000; Kahn and Kenney 1997; but see Koch 1998). The more competitive the election is, the more information is supplied to voters about candidates' policy positions, thereby facilitating policy-based voting. In uncompetitive electoral campaigns in contrast, candidates spend less on their campaigns, and as a result their messages receive less media attention; this in turn limits the supply of policy-based information and contributes to lower levels of programmatic voting. In a similar vein, the extent of polarisation of party positions has been found to elevate the propensity of voters to cast a ballot based on ideological considerations (Ensley 2007; Knutsen and Kumlin 2005; Lachat 2008; van der Eijk *et al.* 2005). When party positions are polarised, information about ideological positions becomes readily available and easier to use. In polarised elections, voters are better able to map their positions onto those of parties. It is important to note that the impact of both electoral competitiveness and party polarisation is mediated through the supply of relevant information to voters. Where relevant electoral information is abundant, voters are more likely to make good decisions.[2]

The literature above was reviewed through the lens of elections as information environments, in their quality of aiding, or potentially burdening, the information acquisition and decision-making of voters. Voters' attributes, such as socioeconomic resources, and contextual attributes, such as the competitiveness of the electoral race, condition the amount of information supplied to voters and the quality of the decisions voters make. Studying elections as information environments helps shift the focus of inquiry from voters and institutions, per se, to the quality and the diffusion of electoral information more broadly. Doing so also helps close in on the principal actors who provide voters with cues in elections – political parties. The following section charts the ways parties help shape the information environments in which voters find themselves.

How parties structure the information environment

Political parties are of primary importance as we try to parse out the quality of electoral information and the effectiveness with which it is diffused. Parties are the actors who, in the process of electoral competition, create a context for voter learning and decision-making. When parties organise the political system effectively, their messages can serve as an important source of information cues that enable reasoned decision-making. When parties fail to send clear signals about their positions, they do not offer the useful information shortcuts voters need to

---

2. An informational argument can be made with regard to voting on retrospective evaluations of the economy. Voting based on economic considerations is fostered when the power of policy making is concentrated, so as to ensure that responsibility for the economy is clear to voters; this in turn facilitates the sanctioning of responsible office-holders for their performance (Aguilar and Sanchez-Cuenca 2008; Anderson 2000; Golder and Stramski 2010; Hellwig 2001; Hellwig and Samuels 2008; Huber and Powell 1994; Lijphart and Aitkin 1994; Nadeau *et al.* 2002; Powell 2009; Powell and Vanberg 2000; Powell and Whitten 1993, p. 199; Samuels and Hellwig 2010; Sanchez-Cuenca 2008).

make decisions. In short, parties shape the quality of the informational environment in which voters find themselves. The point of departure is to understand, first, the functions parties generally have in elections and electoral decision-making, and, second, how instability in political parties may obstruct these functions.

Political analysts as far back as Samuel Huntington have stressed the role of political parties in the functioning of democracy. The representation of citizen interests hinges on political parties; they 'play an exceptional role because most of the time rules of democratic competition enable them to field electoral candidates and coordinate the political actions of legislative representatives as well as government executives' (Kitschelt, Mansfeldova, *et al.* 1999, p. 44). Although parties' procedural role in elections is well recognised, much less has been said about their role in shaping the information environments in which voters operate (for exceptions, see Sniderman 2000; Jackman and Sniderman 2002; Sniderman and Bullock 2004). After all, parties furnish cues to voters, the availability and clarity of which shape the complexity of voters' information environments.

One of the principal functions of political parties in any election is to provide electoral choice sets to voters, or a fixed set of alternatives from which voters can select at the ballot box (Sniderman 2000).[3] These alternatives encompass ideological differences, positions on numerous policy issues, potential coalition partners and the performance records of incumbent parties, to name just a few. Party labels carry 'not only policy information but group alliances, trait judgments, specific examples of group members, and performance assessments' (Rahn 1993, p. 474; cf. Canover and Feldman 1989; Sharp and Lodge 1985). To appreciate the importance of electoral choice sets, one must understand that the electoral alternatives parties present to voters are vast simplifications of the ample information available in the political system around election time. Choice sets can be best understood as ideologically coherent 'bundles' of information which save voters the effort of gathering and then making sense of 'raw' political information (Sniderman 2000). When parties fulfill their informational roles in elections, they successfully structure vast and complex information into a set of manageable electoral alternatives.

How precisely do parties deliver this simplified set of alternatives to voters? For one, parties propose policy remedies to outstanding social, economic and political problems and in doing so limit the number of policy alternatives offered at elections to only a few (Sniderman and Bullock 2004). This simplifies the cognitive task of voters greatly; they need not collect information on social and economic problems or evaluate all potential policy remedies. Beyond identifying social problems and their solutions, parties 'stamp partisan and ideological brands on the arguments offered in their favour' (Sniderman and Bullock 2004, p. 346). In doing so, parties further simplify electoral alternatives by bundling multiple and diverse policy issues into ideologically coherent party programs. As a result

---

3. These alternatives may be termed a 'choice set'. Sniderman (2000, p. 74) defines choice sets as 'the alternatives open to choice' or an 'alternative courses of action framed in terms of government policies'.

of this service to their constituents, voters themselves do not need to coordinate alternatives across issues on the left-right ideological continuum (Jackman and Sniderman 2002). One may also argue that by bundling policy issues into ideologically coherent packages, parties also facilitate the use of ideology as a voting heuristic (Knutsen and Kumlin 2005; Lachat 2008). And by instituting internal discipline, party organisations give voters confidence that individual party members will adhere to broad party platforms.[4] Thus in any given election, parties will ideally deliver a fixed set of alternatives that have been simplified, limited, coherently structured across the ideological spectrum and instituted within the party ranks. By presenting such a set of alternatives to voters, to either accept or reject, political parties greatly lower the barriers to acquiring political information.

An ample literature on voters' use of heuristics finds that by simply paying attention to party cues – that simplified 'choice set' parties present in elections – voters can make reasonably good decisions.[5] Despite a lack of detailed knowledge of parties' policy positions, voters can orient themselves in the policy space when party cues are clear and forthcoming. Information environments, and the parties that structure them, facilitate information seeking by supplying cognitively costless information. The theoretical argument I have laid out is based on the following three tenets: (1) Voters can make reasoned choices because electoral alternatives have been fixed and simplified for them; (2) Political institutions, and above all political parties, structure the electoral choice set; and (3) Voters learning processes and decision outcomes depend on how electoral alternatives have been structured by the party system (Sniderman 2000). Put differently, without electoral choice sets, democratic elections would be unthinkable due to voters' 'informational shortfalls', or the constraints voters face in obtaining and processing full information. In Paul Sniderman's words, voters can rise above their informational deficit 'not because they (mysteriously) can simplify public choices effectively, but because these choices are systematically simplified for them' (2000, p. 81).

In asking if and how parties shape the information environment, this book stands apart from most research in comparative political behaviour which assumes that parties do an equally good job of structuring and communicating information across elections. The question to ask is, under what conditions do parties perform their informational role effectively? That is, when do parties do a good job of simplifying information for voters, and when do they fail their informational role and burden rather than aid decision-making? One could imagine a variety of scenarios from parties repositioning themselves on policy issues or new issues emerging in the course of a campaign to political scandals that take attention away from policy debates. The extent to which parties are

---

4. Indeed, voters seem to take party cohesion into account. It has been shown that when particular candidates take a policy stance that is incongruent with the main party line, voters react accordingly and do not rely on the partisan heuristic to cast a vote (Arceneaux, 2008; but see Dancey and Sheagley 2013).

5. For a recent review of this vast literature, see Carmines and D'Amico (2015).

consistent in their policy stances and the ways in which they communicate these positions through the electoral campaign likely all contribute to the complexity of the information environment. In the section that follows, I examine in depth one such scenario which is not uncommon across democracies – namely, parties reinventing themselves, in part or in full, between elections. I first explain what party instability is and then trace its potential consequences for the information environment and decision-making itself.

Party instability and the information environment

We can imagine multiple ways in which parties can, and often do, transform themselves (Harmel and Janda 1994; Janda 1980). Changes can include the emergence of new parties on the ballot, the disappearance of existing parties, party splits and mergers, the formation of joint lists and pre-electoral coalitions, party name and/or leader changes and possibly others (Mainwaring 1998; Mair 1997; Toole 2000; Shabad and Slomczynski 2004; Kreuzer and Pettai 2003). Such changes are relevant for the information environment in elections because each transformation affects electoral competition and is visible on the electoral ballot, or voters' choice set. As an example, take the 2006 parliamentary election in Italy where several new or changed party formations appeared on the ballot: two Christian democratic parties (CCD and CCU) merged into Union of Christian Democrats and of Centre (UDC); three of the parties (I, PPI and RI) comprising the joint list Margherita merged into a single party of the same name; the pre-electoral alliance Olive Tree changed its name to The Union in 2006. Such changes are important to consider when thinking of voters' information environment because they can, in some instances, drastically and unexpectedly transform the choice sets voters rely on to make decisions. What is more, similar changes in the structure of parties are relatively frequent in modern democracies (Mair *et al.* 2004; Sikk 2005; Sikk 2012; Tavits 2006; Tavits 2008). In understanding how party instability shapes electoral decision-making, we can get a better grasp of electoral politics across a range of democracies.[6]

Party instability puts a question mark over a long-held assumption in comparative political behaviour that the electoral alternatives presented to voters are well-structured and well-defined. Indeed, the extent to which parties are able

---

6. In thinking of elections as information environments, my focus is on party instability that is *externally perceptible*. Changes that are palpable to the voters are more likely to be experienced and to affect information-seeking and decision-making. Internal party transformations, as important as they can be, are likely not visible to the great majority of voters, unless they also manifest externally through structural and/or policy changes. Externally perceptible instability and internal party dynamics are undeniably interconnected. Internal power struggles may lead to party splits, leader changes and the like. Party instability may therefore be a reasonably good indicator of internal party struggles. However, the internal shifts are arguably experienced by voters only when they lead to palpable party change. Such changes are therefore better suited to understanding how party instability shapes the information environments in which voters make electoral choices. Chapter Three offers more details on the concept and empirical operationalisation of party instability.

to fulfil their electoral functions more generally has rarely been scrutinised (for exceptions, see Rohrschneider and Whitefield 2010; Whitefield and Rohrschneider 2009). When parties change repeatedly, they become nothing short of moving targets. Voters must 'construct' the electoral alternatives at their disposal, in the sense of discerning who the new or transformed competitors are and what policy positions they stand for. Party instability further presents a problem of source attribution as the sources of electoral information are unknown or lesser known party organisations. An information environment characterised by party instability presents ill-defined or ill-structured electoral alternatives that need to be sought out by voters. What are the consequences of party instability for voters' information environments?

We can expect party instability to erect informational barriers. Where parties enter the race, voters will have new information to process (e.g., parties' names and leaders) and new information to integrate into their decision-making calculus (e.g., the newcomers' political ideology and levels of competence). Where existing parties transform through mergers and splinters, voters will be faced with the task of tracing new party names and leaders from the earlier organisations to the emerging ones. What is more, many party mergers involve parties that were previously competing against each other.[7] In those cases, voters have the further task of reconciling policy and ideological inconsistencies between the parties comprising the newly merged party organisation. In short, voters will have new and additional information to acquire and digest as the electoral ground shifts under them.

Beyond the sheer amount of additional information voters will face, we can expect that such information be communicated to voters less effectively in elections with new and newly transformed parties than it would be in elections with long-standing and stable parties. The source of information is likely more difficult to attribute when parties are new or newly transformed. Such parties are less familiar to voters than stable parties that have competed over a number of electoral cycles. As a result, the effective communication from new or newly transformed parties to voters may be strained. There is evidence of poor information outcomes in settings where electoral information cannot be easily attributed to a source. A case in point is nonpartisan elections where by definition electoral information is not attributable to any party.[8] In nonpartisan elections, voters have been shown to experience greater difficulty learning about politics (Lupia and McCubbins 1998; Schaffner and Streb 2002). Nonpartisan elections are certainly an extreme example of voters' inability to attribute information to a party. To a lesser degree – and perhaps conditional on the type and sheer amount of party change in a given election – voters will likely also face difficulties in attributing electoral appeals to party sources.

---

7. The exceptions are parties that previously ran as a joint list. Given such parties' history of cooperation, voters should be better able to make sense of the new party merger (e.g., in terms of the congruence of parties' policy positions).

8. Lupia and McCubbins (1998) have called nonpartisan elections 'an example of an institutional environment that hinders reasoned choice' (225).

Party instability is hence likely to (a) increase the amount of new information to be digested by voters and to (b) minimise the effectiveness with which such information is communicated. Together, these effects spell higher informational costs in elections where new or newly transformed parties are abundant. To stay informed, voters would need to devote more resources to acquiring information about new and changing electoral alternatives, including their precious time and cognitive effort. We know that attention to politics is generally scarce due to its high opportunity and transaction costs (Holyoak *et al.* 1989; Kandel *et al.* 1995). Due to the greater amount of new information and parties' lower effectiveness in communicating it, party cues are arguably even more costly to pay attention to and process where parties are unstable. In contributing to a low-information environment in elections, party instability will influence voters' levels of information.

When parties are unstable, they generate a complex, low-information environment in which voters face higher costs and barriers to learning. Clear information is likely harder to come by when parties are new or newly transformed than when parties are stable over time. If instability makes it costlier for voters to acquire electoral information, then those voters embedded in more erratic elections will likely be less familiar with the electoral choice set on offer, including the policy positions of competing parties, than will be voters in elections with long-running, stable parties. The emergence of new parties as well as the transformation of existing parties can make it harder for voters to attribute correctly a set of policy positions to a party. The more instances of party change in a given election, the more attention voters will need to devote to electoral politics in order to keep abreast of party changes and to attribute correctly to parties their respective choice sets. Hence, one empirical implication of the theoretical framework outlined above is that voters will be less familiar with party positions, particularly as instability rises.[9] This implication is developed further and tested empirically in Chapter Four. In leaving voters with less and less clear electoral information, party instability is also likely to shape the way in which voters make decisions – a question I examine in the following section.

How voters cope with party instability: Heuristics for unstable parties

The literature on electoral decision-making reviewed thus far has developed out of electoral contexts where the alternatives presented to the voter are well-structured and well-defined. In such a framework, and without regard for types of electoral institutions or voters' levels of political sophistication, the alternatives on the ballot are assumed to be fixed and presented as such to the decision-maker (Langley *et al.* 1987; Lau 2003). When parties are unstable, however, they generate a complex

---

9.   In some cases, voters also face higher *opportunities* to become informed in elections of high party instability. Indeed this was arguably the case in two elections with extremely high instability (in Poland and Bulgaria). The transforming electoral landscape received ample media attention – as in part attested to by high electoral turnout – thus compensating for the higher informational barriers. See Chapter Four for further discussion of these cases.

information environment characterised by ill-defined or ill-structured alternatives that need to be sorted out by the decision-maker. The literature has thus far not grappled with this problem; we have rather assumed that electoral alternatives are equally well defined and continuous over electoral cycles and that voters draw on their stored knowledge of party positions, even in low-information elections. The following quote from McDermott (1998, p. 898) represents this view:

> In low information elections, most voters inadvertently obtain basic information about the candidates, such as party identification and incumbent/ challenger status. Consequently, *through past experience and stored knowledge*, a voter can associate a candidate with a political and/or social group and project onto the candidate such things as the issue positions they believe the group holds, or the political performance associated with that group. [Emphasis added]

In contrast to voting for long-running, continuous parties, voters confronted with new or newly transformed parties have little past experience or stored knowledge to draw on. It is therefore an open question how voters make decisions in elections where the electoral alternatives are fluid and must be sought out. In considering the role of party instability in electoral decision-making, the following section seeks to shed light on how decision-making processes unfold in less well-structured electoral spaces. Namely, how do voters decide between the party alternatives on offer? How do voters cope with the scarcity of electoral information? What decision-making strategies do they use to adapt to low-information environments?

The literature in cognitive psychology offers some preliminary answers to these questions. The information environment in which voters find themselves has been shown to influence more than just voters' familiarity with political parties; it can also shape the ways in which voters make decisions. Cognitive psychologists have identified two distinct processing modes which manifest themselves depending on the amount of information the decision-maker has (Bargh 1999; Eagly and Chaiken 1999; Giner-Sorolla 1999; Petty and Cacioppo 1986). When decision-makers have plenty of information at their disposal, they engage in central route processing or a 'relatively analytic and comprehensive treatment of judgment-relevant information' (Chen and Chaiken 1999, p. 74). In electoral decision-making, voters would make the cognitive effort to process political parties' programmatic appeals and judge systematically their congruence with their own policy positions. In contrast when decision-makers either lack information or motivation to process new information, they will engage in peripheral processing or heuristics processing which is routine and relatively effortless (Petty and Cacioppo 1986; Eagly and Chaiken 1999). When it comes to electoral decision-making, voters processing information in the second mode would rely on simple heuristics (e.g., personal feelings towards candidates) rather than systematically judge policy congruence between parties' stances and their own positions.

Dual-processing theories have developed out of cognitive psychology with an interest in the impact of decision-makers' individual attributes on the information-processing modes employed. Studies in political psychology have also contributed to this research by tracing the effects of individuals' motivation and cognitive capacity to process new information on the ways in which political decisions are made (Basinger and Lavine, 2005; Gomez and Wilson, 2001; Lavine and Gschwend, 2007; Rahn, 1993; Singh and Roy 2014). Apart from individual attributes, there is accumulating evidence that the information environment itself influences the processing mode decision-makers employ. The relative familiarity and safety of the environment can influence decision-makers' emotional state of mind and cause them to shift processing modes (Marcus *et al.* 2000; Marcus and MacKuen 1993). Encounters with information that is incongruent with previously held beliefs can trigger emotional dissonance and shift the decision-maker's processing mode from routine and relatively effortless to one where information is considered carefully (Lodge and Taber 2000; Redlawsk 2001). Beyond the type of information supplied, its sheer amount in a given context can influence the processing mode decision-makers employ. In elections where party positions are polarised, information about parties' ideology is more easily accessible to voters; this in turn triggers careful processing of ideological information and results in higher rates of programmatic voting (Ensley 2007; Lachat 2008). A similar logic applies to the competitiveness of the electoral race (Basinger and Lavine 2005; Gronke 2000).

In accordance with the quality of the information environment voters find themselves in, they will employ more or less cognitively demanding strategies to decide between parties (cf. Chaiken 1980; Maheswaran and Chaiken 1991). Voters embedded in high-information environments are more likely to employ diagnostic criteria, such as parties' policy positions, and engage in more effortful decision-making by comparing systematically their positions to those of competing parties (Ensley 2007; Lachat 2008; Lavine and Gschwend 2007; Rahn 1993). Where information is scarce or ineffectively communicated, voters will rely on simpler and cognitively less costly criteria to decide. Rahn (1993, p. 475) put it as follows: '...individuals are viewed as flexible information processors... In low-motivation settings or when information costs are high, individuals may choose to use a less expensive, theory-based processing strategy (e.g., a heuristic).' In a series of studies, McDermott (1997, 1998) found empirical support for this claim; when information about candidates was costlier to acquire, gender and ethnic stereotypes of candidates factored increasingly into voters' decisions. Similarly, when voters lacked knowledge about candidates' policy positions, they were likely to rely on their stereotypes based on the candidate's party affiliation (Conover and Feldman 1982). Which decision-making criteria voters employ – policy-based evaluations or candidate stereotypes – depends in part on the quality of the information environment in which voters are embedded.

In impeding parties from effectively structuring the information environment for voters, I have argued that party instability is likely to have a direct effect on the availability and clarity of electoral information. Thus far, we do not have any real notion of the kinds of decision-making rules voters use when the electoral choice set before the voter is unstable between elections. Recall that in elections with party instability, voters are asked to do more of the work in terms of acquiring, attributing and processing electoral information, likely resulting in lower information levels. As many studies in cognitive and political psychology have demonstrated, when voters lack knowledge of the electoral choice set before them, they are less likely to decide based on information-rich diagnostic criteria and are more likely to rely instead on cognitively less costly criteria. This literature therefore offers an important preliminary insight as to how voters will cope with the electoral complexity generated by party instability – namely, by adopting cognitively less taxing decision-making strategies.

While dual-processing theories bear on how voters decide in low-information elections, it is important to consider the specific effects of fluid electoral choice-sets on electoral decision-making. While it is reasonable to expect that some low-information heuristics are applied more frequently when parties are unstable (e.g., feelings towards party leaders), I argue that party instability challenges the logic of other low-information decision-making mechanisms (e.g., economic voting), which are less likely to be employed as parties change. Still, party instability may trigger its own unique set of coping heuristics (what I label the 'party instability heuristic') to help voters minimise uncertainty and make a reasoned vote choice. I examine a series of low-information heuristics in turn as they apply when the electoral choices sets before voters are unstable.

The first decision-making strategy I examine is programmatic voting based on policy and ideological appeals. Following dual-processing theories, we can expect voters to be less likely to vote on programmatic considerations because they simply lack a clear notion of the policy choice set before them when parties are unstable. As I argue in Chapter Five, this line of reasoning may be overly simplistic. I contend that voters will take into account party positions but will do so in different ways for parties that are new or newly transformed and for those that are established. When voting for stable parties, voters are more likely to base their decisions on programmatic appeals as per standard theories of proximity voting (Downs 1954). As such theories require higher levels of information, they are more likely to apply to stable, long-running parties.

In contrast, when parties are unstable, a less cognitively costly mechanism of programmatic voting is likely to unravel. The direction-intensity model of voting developed by Rabinowitz and MacDonald (1989) requires considerably less information on the part of voters. Voters need only discern the direction of the party's ideology (e.g., either left or right) and have a sense of the intensity with which the party advocates for its position rather than pinpoint each party's exact set of policy positions. This alternative decision-making model is also based on programmatic appeals, but it has a considerably lower informational threshold. In Chapter Five, I argue that direction-intensity voting may be one adaptive strategy of voting in complex electoral spaces where stable parties compete along new or newly transformed organisations.

Another decision-making rule which is central to understanding electoral behaviour and which has been lauded for its low-information rationality is the economic vote (Key 1966; Fiorina 1981; Basinger and Lavine 2005).

In contrast to a proximity voter who would need to seek information about each party's policy positions and then exert the cognitive effort to estimate distances between party positions and his own, the economic voter casts a ballot either for or against the incumbent based on one simple piece of information – the state of the economy. Against this conventional 'low-information' wisdom, I argue in Chapter Six that effective economic voting requires not only information about the state of the economy but also voters' judgments of whether or not such information is a good predictor of future governing capacity and performance. In this regard, information on changes in party organisation is key to shaping voter assessments of parties' future governing competences and may in fact override pure economic evaluations. I argue that the stability of the electoral choice set conditions the viability of economic voting as a decision-making rule and that economic voting may not be an optimal strategy when parties change between elections. Party instability thus challenges the universal desirability of economic voting across elections. Contrary to what the conventional wisdom on the low-information rationality of economic voting would suggest, I argue instead that economic voting is not an optimal coping mechanism for fluid electoral choice sets.

Programmatic and retrospective considerations are just two of an array of decision-making rules voters can rely on. In addition, I examine two heuristics that can prove useful to voters in low-information elections. The first such rule is valence appeals based on voters' feelings towards party leaders (Bean and Mughan 1989; Cain et al. 1987; Canover and Feldman 1989; Kaase 1994; Karvonen 2010). Leader effects are plausible in low-information spaces for two reasons. First like direction-intensity rules, personality appeals require considerably lower levels of information. Voters need little, if any, information on parties' policy positions. They can simply decide based on their gut feelings towards political personalities. Second, some scholars have argued that because new parties lack social roots, they are less likely to be embedded in the traditional social cleavages of a given electorate and will instead run on salient political personalities (Grofman et al. 2000; Ramonaitė 2007). While anecdotal evidence of this is abundant, thus far we lack a formal test of the strength of leader effects for new and transformed parties. Indeed, given the mixed evidence produced by the literature on the personalisation of politics (cf. Karvonen 2010), party instability could serve as an important moderating factor that can help explain puzzling variation across elections.

Finally, I consider the extent to which information about a party's history of instability can in and of itself serve voters to adapt to a complex and uncertain electoral space. Whether parties are new or newly transformed, they present voters with considerable uncertainty about their policy commitments and competence. Risk-averse voters may consequently avoid new and unstable parties as a rule. The 'party instability heuristic', as I label it, is essentially a voting strategy of minimising risk and uncertainty (cf. Alvarez 1998; Koch 2003). The use of party instability as a heuristic is not incompatible with recent evidence that voters tend to avoid parties whose policy positions are uncertain (Ezrow et al. 2014). However, evidence from case studies in post-socialist democracies suggests instead that, all else equal, voters are in fact attracted to newcomers (Sikk 2012). I parse between these conflicting arguments in Chapter Five.

Contribution to extant theory

The theoretical framework and its empirical implications outlined in this chapter contribute to at least two distinct literatures in political science: the mechanisms of electoral decision-making and political representation more broadly (e.g., Baldassarri 2013; Dalton, Farrell and McAllister 2011; Duch and Stevenson 2008; Ezrow 2010; Lenz 2013; Lau and Redlawsk 2006; Rohrschneider and Whitefield 2013). The book shares many scholars' preoccupation with the quality of electoral decision-making and political representation and examines similarly the ideological congruence between parties and their voters, the strength of economic voting and the acquisition of electoral information by voters. After all, the presence of free and competitive elections, without further stipulation, does not tell us much about the quality of democratic representation (Mill 1958; Roberts 2009). Elections are meaningful as long as they provide representation to citizens; they are the tool citizens use to elect politicians who represent their policy preferences and to sanction those who do not perform satisfactorily. How voters make decisions at elections is essential to understanding the linkages between voters and parties and the quality of electoral democracy.

While extant research has thoroughly investigated individual and macro-institutional explanations of electoral choice, my book centres on the mediators between citizens and policy makers – political parties (Kelsen 1929 (cited in Samuels and Hellwig (2010)), Powell 2000, 2004). I have argued that this focus is justified due to the important – though often neglected – *informational* roles parties perform in elections. Indeed, parties are the principal actors to organise ample and often complex information in a manageable set of alternatives for voters to choose from. In the process of electoral competition, parties further communicate the alternatives they offer to voters and facilitate the acquisition of new information. In line with the important contributions by Paul Sniderman and his coauthors, I shift attention away from individual and institutional factors and stress instead the role of political parties in structuring the electoral information environments in which voters find themselves. What is critical for reasoned decision-making is not only the degree to which voters can process electoral information but also, and perhaps more importantly, the availability and usefulness of the party cues on which voters rely to elect policymakers (Sniderman 2000). Studying the vote choice through the lens of parties' informational roles will help take a fresh look at standard theories of vote choice.

In an important way, this contribution departs from the extant literature in electoral behavior. It analyses empirically the unstated assumption that the electoral alternatives presented to voters are equally well-structured and unvarying across elections (c.f. Carmines and D'Amico 2015; Langley *et al.* 1987; Lau 2003). The literature reviewed here has thus far not addressed (a) whether or not the electoral choice set is equally 'fixed' across electoral cycles or (b) how decision-making proceeds in information environments where the alternatives are less structured and more fluid over time. I have argued that party instability offers one scenario in which the electoral alternatives are non-fixed and where voters need to exert some cognitive effort in making out the menu of parties at the ballot box. Indeed instability in political parties is just one possible destabilising factor when it comes to electoral competition; shifting policy positions during the course of an electoral campaign is another potential source of fluid electoral alternatives (c.f. Hellwig 2012; Dalton and McAllister 2015). This book takes just a brief glimpse into the Pandora's Box of ill-structured electoral choice sets. In doing so, I hope it inspires further research on how voters choose in low-information environments and what the consequences are for broader political representation and accountability.

In considering the role of party instability in shaping the information environment, this book brings the electoral manoeuvring of political parties to the centre of vote choice (e.g., Hellmann 2011; Rose and Munro 2009; Spirova 2007; Tavits 2013). Understanding the power of party organisations to facilitate, or stymie, political representation promises to contribute to our knowledge of the workings and potential pitfalls of representative democracy. Re-examining the vote through the lens of party instability allows me to investigate the extent to which organisational changes in parties upset the quality of electoral decision-making and modern European democracy more broadly. As such, this project goes beyond the institutions which merely guarantee the presence of electoral democracy and examines the degree to which citizens rule under unstable parties. In doing so, I am able to inform current theories of information-seeking and decision-making in elections and to strengthen our extant knowledge of political representation.

An empirical observation – that there is significant cross-election variation in how well electoral alternatives are organised and communicated to voters – drives the analyses pursued in the chapters to follow. Political parties vary in their longevity and stability; many party organisations are short-lived, with newcomers coming and going, while existing parties reshuffle and transform. The ins and outs of party dynamics are explored in the following chapter. Such instability in parties may have thus far unexplored consequences for the ability of voters to acquire new information. I have argued that when parties change repeatedly or come and go, they raise the costs of obtaining information by, in part, making it harder for voters to attribute correctly cues to changing parties. In the three empirical chapters that follow, I test how the quality of the information environment created by party instability shapes information seeking and decision-making. In the first empirical chapter (Chapter Four), I test the extent to which voters face higher costs to information in elections where parties are new or transformed. I then examine decision-making heuristics under unstable parties and their implications for political representation and accountability. In Chapter Five, I examine the electoral considerations voters use when choosing stable and unstable parties, respectively. In the final empirical chapter, I test the extent to which voters are able to sanction incumbents as they transform. To understand how the quality of information across elections conditions voting behaviour, I test the empirical implications of my argument by comparing party manoeuvring and voter decision-making across a range of European democracies.

Chapter Three

Electoral Instability in Parties: Concept, Measurement and Dynamics

Party system instability consists of changes in the patterns of interaction between parties and the electorate (Pedersen 1979, p.4). Even so, the study of party system instability has by and large focused on change originating from shifts in voter preferences, as evinced by the prevalent use of the Pedersen index of electoral volatility (e.g., Korasteleva 2000; Lane 2008; Mainwaring 1998; Mainwaring and Zoco 2007; Robbins and Hunter 2012). This is to the neglect of electoral changes in parties, including their ideology, structure and strategies. Party change is an important component of party system change not only because parties are the building blocks of party systems, but also because party change is a defining characteristic of most electoral landscapes (Bielasiak 2002; Maguire 1983; Mair *et al.* 2004; Tavits 2008).

The nearly exclusive focus on voter volatility in the study of party systems is compounded further by conceptual and empirical problems. Existing measures of voter volatility have often been used as akin to instability in parties and party systems despite their original formulation as vote transfers between elections (e.g., Bielasiak 1997; Bielasiak 2002; Evans 2002; Maguire 1983; Mainwaring and Zoco 2007; Taagepera and Grofman 2003). Closely related is a well-recognised empirical limitation of such indicators – namely, their inability to incorporate electoral changes in parties (Birch 2001; Powell and Tucker 2014; Sikk 2005). The entry and exit of parties is an impediment to estimating voter volatility, forcing scholars to ignore changes and/or continuities in the evolution of parties (for an overview, see Sikk 2005). Disregarding instability in political parties becomes especially problematic in some new democracies where such changes are endemic (Bielasiak 2002; Tavits 2008). Extending the use of voter volatility indicators to developing party systems proliferates conceptual stretching and obfuscates the nature of systemic instability.

This chapter develops an empirical indicator of instability in political parties based on six categories of electoral change in parties: the emergence of new parties, the disbanding of existing parties, the formation of party mergers, splinter parties and party entry into and exit from joint lists. The complexity of such changes usually means that they are studied qualitatively and cannot be readily integrated in empirical models (e.g., Birch 1998; Kreuzer and Pettai 2003; Mainwaring and Torcal 2006; Panebianco 1988; Protsyk and Wilson 2003; Shabad and Slomczynski 2004). Hence in addition to the rich party-level data, I offer an aggregate indicator of party instability at the election level of analysis.

The indicators of party change and accompanying data (twenty-seven European democracies, 1987–2011) enable me to investigate empirically the interplay between political elites and masses in chapters that follow.

Party system change: concept and existing indicators

Party system change is 'the total set of changes in patterns of interaction and competition' at the levels of political parties and the electorate as well as between them (Pedersen 1979, p.4).[1] Change in party systems is thus effected by parties, the electorate, institutions and their interaction (Smith 1989). Change stemming from the electorate has been the dominant approach in studying party system change, to the neglect of other aspects, including change in party structure (Mair 1989).[2] In this section, I review existing indicators of party system change, discuss their limitations and recent modifications and chart new paths for measuring electoral change in parties. The most widely used measure of party system change is the Pedersen index of volatility (Pedersen 1979). In its original formulation, the index was intended to account for party system instability attributable to individual vote transfers between elections, admittedly to the neglect of change at 'the level of the party as an organisation' (Pedersen 1979, p. 4). However, many studies treat volatility as akin to instability in parties and party systems at large (e.g., Bielasiak 1997; Bielasiak 2002; Evans 2002; Maguire 1983; Taagepera and Grofman 2003). Rarely is it recognised that the index conflates the roles of elites and masses in destabilising party systems, or that this conflation impedes understanding the nature of party system change (for exceptions, see Birch 2001; Mair 1997; Powell and Tucker 2014; Tavits 2008). This is because the index is ill-suited to measure electoral changes in parties. Gaging volatility in multi-party systems with changing parties requires not only researching how parties emerge, disappear, merge and split, but also deciding how to deal with party change in estimating volatility (for a discussion, see Powell and Tucker 2014). As Pedersen's index was not developed to accommodate changes in parties, they are relegated to an 'other' category, and researchers are forced either to ignore them (e.g., treat splinters as a continuation

---

1. Like Pedersen (1979), I conceptualise party system change as a characteristic in magnitude of any continuous party system. Party systems are, to varying degrees, undergoing changes due to turnover in parties and shifting voter preferences. To convey this, I use the term party system instability. I therefore do not conceptualise party system change as one of a type which would imply 'transformation of the direction of competition or the governing formula' (Mair 1989, p.257). A party system change of this magnitude occurred in Italy in the early 1990s (see Morlino 1996).

2. The dominant focus on the electorate is not without problems: it suggests that party systems change only when there is evidence of the electorate's shifting preferences and that the absence of electoral change is indicative of party and party system stability (Mair 1989). Some democracies of Southern and Central and Eastern Europe, for example, offer ample evidence of party and party system change despite stability in electoral preferences (Barnes et al. 1985; Tavits 2008a).

of preexisting parties) or to disregard continuities between past and present parties (e.g., treat splinters as new parties) (for a discussion, see Sikk 2005). The problem becomes all the more acute in developing democracies with frequent party change.

In recognising the conceptual and empirical challenges presented by the volatility index, recent efforts have centred on isolating the portion of volatility attributable to party change (Birch 2001; Rose and Mishler 2010; Powell and Tucker 2014; Sikk 2005). One approach has been to estimate separately the vote shares of existing and new parties (Birch 2001; Rose and Mishler 2010; Sikk 2005; Tavits 2008) while others have partitioned volatility ex post facto into its component parts (Powell and Tucker 2014). With both approaches, scholars aim to approximate the portions of change in election results due to electoral instability in parties and due to vote transfers among stable parties, respectively. Importantly, these new measures record the effects of party change as reflected in election results rather than the sheer prevalence of instability in parties.[3]

The literature has also produced several indicators of change in party organisations. Among them are party discipline, party personalism, the percentage of independent candidates, the extent of candidate party switching and the affiliation patterns of politicians (Birch 1998; Dix 1992; Kreuzer and Pettai 2003; Mainwaring and Torcal 2006; Panebianco 1988; Protsyk and Wilson 2003; Shabad and Slomczynski 2004). These measures have been partial, in documenting only some aspects of change, and have been limited to a handful of cases, thus limiting replicability and cross-national comparability.

Finally, it is worth stressing the continuous interaction between the multiple components of party systems. While the Pedersen index has often been criticised for confounding electoral shifts with changes in parties (Birch 2001; Mair 1997; Powell and Tucker 2014), the two sources of change are interdependent and it is therefore empirically difficult to tease them apart. On one hand, voter utility for a given party depends on the characteristics of all parties (Alvarez and Nagler 1998; Quinn *et al.* 1999), arguably including their instability. As I show in Chapter Five, party instability influences voters' electoral choice. On the other hand, party changes are at least partially motivated by shifts, or expected shifts, in voter preferences. While it is difficult to separate the two sources of party system instability entirely, we can limit their conflation by discontinuing the reliance on the Pedersen index as an indicator of party or party system change and by excluding election results from estimates of party instability. The following section formally introduces the concept of electoral instability in parties and proposes a set of empirical indicators to estimate it.

---

3. Furthermore, these new approaches estimate instability only partially, neglecting the full array of possible party changes. Sikk (2005) and Tavits (2008) estimate electoral shifts among new parties alone, to the exclusion of other types of party change. O'Dwyer (2004) and Toole (2000) similarly consider only new parties and disbanded parties in estimating party system instability.

Electoral instability in parties: concept and measurement

Electoral instability in parties: concept

The interaction of parties and their responses to electoral and institutional change are an important component of systemic instability (Smith 1989). While multiple types of party change are conceivable (e.g., changes in party ideology, strategy or structure), this inquiry focuses on structural changes in parties that are consequential for electoral competition (Harmel and Janda 1994; Janda 1980). Such changes are important to consider when thinking of voters' information environment because they have the potential to transform the choice sets voters rely on to make decisions and to do so drastically and unexpectedly. What is more, organisational changes in the structure of parties are relatively frequent in modern democracies. Understanding how party instability shapes electoral decision-making, we can get a better grasp of electoral politics across a range of democracies. Here I discuss the nature of party change, the unit of analysis in conceptualising and measuring it and its relationship to party system change.

Having conceptualised elections as information environments in Chapter Two, my focus is on *externally perceptible* changes in party organisations. Changes that are visible to voters are much more likely to affect electoral information-seeking and decision-making than are behind-the-scene internal struggles. The latter are likely not visible to the great majority of voters unless they also manifest externally through structural and/or policy changes (e.g., when internal power struggles result in a splinter party). Externally perceptible instability and internal party dynamics are undeniably interconnected, but the internal shifts are arguably experienced by voters only when they lead to palpable party change. External organisational changes are therefore better suited to understanding how party instability shapes the information environments in which voters make electoral choices. Changes in party structure that are visible on the electoral ballot include the emergence of new parties, the disappearance of existing parties, party splinters and mergers, and/or the formation and disbanding of joint lists (Mainwaring 1998; Mair 1997; Toole 2000; Shabad and Slomczynski 2004; Kreuzer and Pettai 2003).

By nature party changes are not incidental. Parties are conservative organisations unlikely to undertake changes to their structure as this requires building a coalition of support within the organisation and overcoming resistance from party members (Harmel and Janda 1994). It is important to emphasise that while party changes are not incidental, they may be haphazard. Party changes are not necessarily incremental, gradual or leading to a certain outcome (e.g., party institutionalisation) but potentially abrupt, discontinuous and chaotic (Harmel and Janda 1994; Panebianco 1988). External factors, such as electoral rules, and/or internal dynamics, such as change of the dominant faction within the party, can act as catalysts for a process that culminates in party change (Harmel and Janda 1994; Sikk 2005; Tavits 2006; Tavits 2008).

There are at least three possible units of analysis when studying party change: coalitions of individuals (e.g., Birch 1998; Shabad and Slomczynski

2004); coalitions of factions (e.g., Protsyk and Wilson 2003); and parties of a divisive nature (Laver 1989). I contend that using the third approach is optimal. It retains the party, rather than individuals or factions, as the fundamental unit of analysis; in doing so, it avoids tracing a potentially infinite number of changes among politicians, cross-cutting factions and/or sub-factions. Conceiving of the party as potentially divisive allows for conflict within parties over time instead of assuming that parties are static, unitary actors. By giving consideration to intra-party politics, we can trace changes in the structure of party organisations, such as party splits and fusions.

Finally, what does party change mean for party system instability? Mair (1989) was sceptical about the study of party change as an indicator of party system change because the former does not necessarily matter for the latter.[4] However, a similar argument may be made about the significance of voter fluctuations for party system change as the former does not necessarily indicate a party system transformation, such as an electoral realignment. Notwithstanding Mair's observation, changes in parties have important implications for electoral competition. As I have argued in Chapter Two, some stability in electoral alternatives facilitates the communication of party cues to voters. Parties have a central role in organising electoral information for voters. The empirical chapters offer considerable evidence to suggest that high party instability is consequential for voter familiarity with electoral alternatives and the vote itself.

Measuring electoral instability in parties

I use six indicators to operationalise electoral changes in parties: the emergence of new parties, the disbanding of existing parties, splinter parties, party mergers, entrance in and exit from party joint lists (Mair 1997; Toole 2000; Shabad and Slomczynski 2004; Kreuzer and Pettai 2003).[5] I document such changes in each party organisation between two subsequent elections (at times $t-1$ and t) at the party level of analysis. All parties with at least five per cent of the vote in any lower-house parliamentary election form part of the dataset.[6] The threshold excludes marginal, non-parliamentary parties that were not adequately covered in the press or by secondary sources. Categories of party change are not exclusive. I discuss the coding of each variable below, with illustrative examples from the dataset.[7]

---

4. Recall that Mair's conceptualisation of party system change is one of type, not of magnitude.

5. Joining and leaving party lists do not change the structure of parties as they maintain considerable organisational independence even as they appear on the same electoral ballot. However, when parties join or leave party lists, they alter the menu of voting alternatives, much like party mergers and splinters (see Table 2). Furthermore, parties use the electoral strategies of mergers and joint lists interchangeably depending on the incentive structures created by electoral institutions. Before the 1998 election in Slovakia, for example, we observe a flurry of mergers that can be attributed to the steeper electoral threshold that was passed for joint lists.

6. See the Appendix for details on the inclusion threshold.

7. To compile the data, I used multiple secondary sources as described in the Appendix.

New Party. A party is coded as new at election *t* if it had not competed in election *t-1*; the indicator is binary where a new party is coded 1 and existing parties are coded as 0. My goal was to code truly new party formations. Parties that originated from mergers, splits or joint lists of existing parties at *t-1* are not coded as new party formations (Barnea and Rahat 2011; Sikk 2005). For example, Democrats for Strong Bulgaria first competed independently in the 2005 election but is not coded as new because it originated in a 2004 splinter of the United Democratic Forces. In the Netherlands, Martin Batenburg founded the General Elderly Alliance which gained six seats in the 1994 election. The party is coded new because it had no links to pre-existing organisations.

Disbanded Party. If a party at *t-1* did not appear for re-election at *t*, it is coded as disbanded (and assigned a value of 1; 0 otherwise). Similarly to the previous category, parties that appear for re-election at t as mergers, splinters or on joint lists are not considered disbanded. Parties that received a small per centage of the electoral vote at *t-1* were most likely to disband. Examples include Slovenia is Ours, the Danish Centre of Democrats the Liberal Party of Italy and the Belgian ROSSEM.

Splinter. If a party at *t* is a new formation that formed after its members split off from an existing party, it is coded as a splinter party (and assigned a value of 1; 0 otherwise). Defection of party members that did not result in a new party at *t* is not considered a splinter. For example, the Czech Freedom Union is a splinter from the Civic Democratic Party. Right of the Republic, a 2007 splinter of the Polish Law and Justice, is not coded as it did not meet the inclusion threshold.

Merged. If a party from *t-1* officially merged with at least one other party at *t*, it is coded as merged (and assigned a value of 1; 0 otherwise). Each party that participated in a merger is coded separately. The defection of party members from one party to another is not considered a merger between two parties. For example, a four-party merger in Iceland resulted in the founding of the Social Democratic Alliance in 2000. The 1999 merger between the Irish Democratic Left and the Labour Party is not included in the index as the former party did not meet the 5 per cent inclusion threshold.

Joint lists (two indicators: entry and exit). Entry is coded 1 if a party at *t-1* appears at *t* on an electoral ballot with at least one other party; exit is coded 1 if a party at *t* no longer appears on a joint list; 0 otherwise. A joint list comprises of two or more parties that compete on a single electoral ticket; the parties remain organisationally independent. For example, the joint list L'Ulivo, compromising the Democrats of the Left, the Movement of European Republicans and Daisy-Democracy, gained 31 per cent of the vote in the 2006 Italian election. Parties that did not participate on joint lists or remained on the same joint lists are coded as 0, such as the long-term joint list, Democratic Unity Coalition, between the Portuguese Communist Party and The Greens. Each party that participated in a joint list is coded separately. Pre-electoral coalitions (in which parties agree to form a government after the election or coordinate opposition efforts) are not joint lists as the parties do not run on the same ticket; membership in pre-electoral or governing coalitions is not taken into account when coding joint lists.

Based on the six indicators above, I have compiled a party-level dataset of changes in parties from twenty-seven European democracies: seventeen West European and ten Central and East European democracies, 1987–2011 (148 elections).[8] The elections from Central and Eastern Europe span the ten continuously democratic polities since 1989, and the data on Western Europe matches this time period. Unlike existing indices of party change (e.g., Birch 2001; Sikk 2005), the data set incorporates elections from both mature and developing democracies and thus allows for comparison and robustness checks across regions. This is especially important given evidence of the different patterns and nature of party system change across established and less consolidated party systems (e.g., Bielasiak 2002; Tavits 2008). Figure 3.1 attests to these differences. In both Central and Eastern Europe and in Western Europe, parties are most often destabilised by entry in and exit from joint lists and entry in mergers; in absolute terms, however, in WE such changes are much less frequent. In CEE on average 28 per cent of parties per election enter into a joint list with another party and another 17 per cent abandon the joint list by the following election. The formation of new parties and the disappearance of parties are the least common forms of party change in both regions.

An election-level index

To gain a sense of overall instability in parties between two elections, this chapter proposes an index of change in political parties at the election level of analysis. While the detailed data described above records the types of instability occurring in each party, the index aims to measure overall instability in parties between subsequent elections. For this purpose, the overall indicator records the number of new or modified party formations between elections t and $t-1$. I estimate an aggregate index of party change based on the six categories of change. Electoral Instability in Parties at election t (EIP_t) is a simple, additive index of the six categories of party change that occur between subsequent elections $t-1$ and t for all parties that pass the 5 per cent threshold.[9]

To illustrate the coding of EIP, I describe how EIP varied over time in four countries. I trace EIP levels in four cases: Belgium, Italy, Estonia and Poland

---

8.   See Table A.1 in the Appendix for a list of elections.

9.   See the Appendix for details on how the 5 per cent threshold is applied to mergers and joint lists.

Figure 3.1: Per cent of parties changing in an average election, by type of instability and region

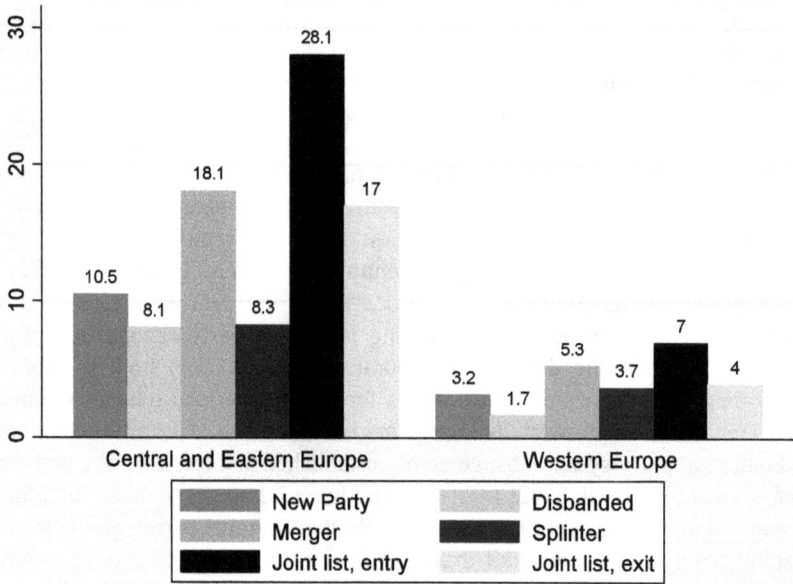

(*see* Figure 3.2). The four countries experienced elections with some of the highest EIP scores in WE and CEE, respectively, though trends over time vary drastically across the four countries. Belgium is relatively stable, with an occasional peak in EIP. Estonia experienced extremely high instability in the early elections after independence but exhibits a clear pattern of decline. In Poland and Italy, EIP varies substantially without a consistent pattern.

The first panel in Figure 3.2 shows EIP levels in Belgium. Instability in Belgium is relatively low, save for a peak in 2003 when the Belgian party system experienced a number of party changes. Between 1999 and 2003, the conservative People's Union (VU) produced two splinter parties: Spirit (14.9 per cent in 2003) and the New Flemish Alliance (3.1 per cent); each of the VU splinters had abandoned the VU-ID21 joint list they ran on in 1999.[10] Spirit and the Flemish Socialist Party then ran on a joint list together (14.9 per cent). The Liberal Reformation Party and the Francophone Democratic Front merged into the Reformist Movement (14.1 per cent). The splinter that passed the 5 per cent threshold, the new joint list, the disbanded joint lists and the new merger resulted in an EIP score of four for the 2003 election.

---

10. Note that changes in the New Flemish Alliance (splinter and joint list exit) are not recorded in the party-level data set because the party did not pass the 5 per cent threshold in 2003.

Figure 3.2: EIP time series for Belgium, Italy, Estonia and Poland

Electoral instability in parties

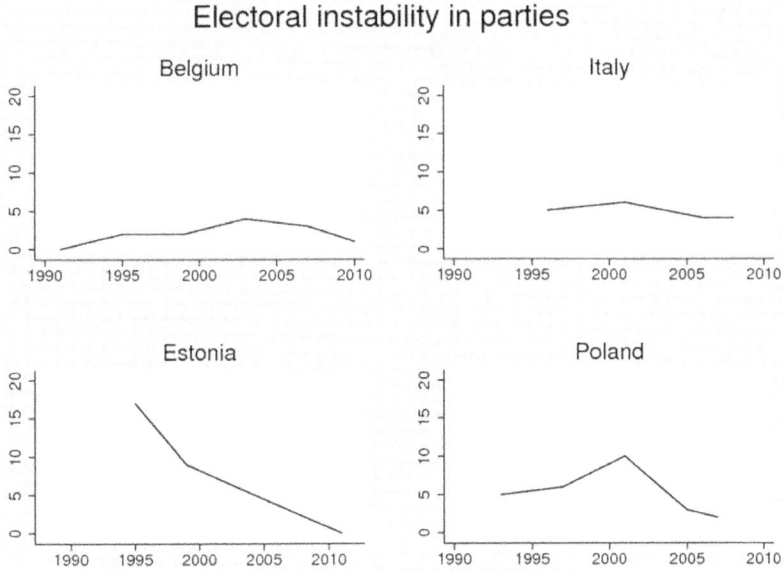

In Western Europe, the party system most vulnerable to change is Italy, experiencing an average EIP score of 4.75 between 1994 and 2008. The time series for Italy begin in 1994 due to the dramatic changes the party system underwent in the late 1980s and early 1990s (see Morlino 1996).[11] Instability in Italy is rarely driven by the emergence of new parties or by the disbanding of existing ones; rather, parties continuously fuse, split and drift in and of out of joint lists.[12] Observers of Italian elections can confirm that such instability is not trivial. Compare the list of party alternatives in the two most recent Italian elections in the data set (Table 3.1). While not a single party was either new or had disbanded between 2006 and 2008, the party alternatives look altogether different. Given how different party alternatives were in 2006 and 2008, many

---

11. Using EIP, or for that matter electoral volatility, to account for *systemic* changes in a party system is misleading, as we are arguably not dealing with the same continuous party system.

12. Italian party systems often experience another level of complexity – changes in pre-electoral coalitions (e.g., Casa delle Liberta) – which is not taken into account here. Unlike parties comprising a joint list or a merger, parties forming a pre-electoral coalition do *not* run on the same electoral ticket and consequently changes in pre-electoral coalitions are not reflected on ballots.

Table 3.1: Electoral alternatives in Italy: 2006 and 2008 elections

2006 Party Alternatives	2008 Party Alternatives
Lega Nord – MpA	Lega Nord (LN)
Union of Christian Democrats and Democrats of Centre (UDCe)	Democratic Union of Centre (UDCe)
Forza Italia (FI)	Il Popolo della Liberta (PdL)
DC-Nuovo PSI	La Destra – Fiamma Tricolore
National Alliance (AN)	Il Popolo della Liberta (PdL)
L'Ulivo	Democratic Party (PD) /Popolo della Liberta (PdL)
Communist Refoundation Party (RC)	La Sinistra - l'Arcobaleno

Note: LN had ran on a joint list with the Movement for Autonomy in 2006 but ran separately in 2008. UDCe produced a splinter that contested the election on the PdL joint list in 2008, along with FI, AN and DC-Nuovo PSI (a marginal 2006 joint list of Socialist and Christian Democrats). L'Ulivo produced a merger, PD, that ran independently, and a splinter, LD, that ran on the PdL list. RC ran on a single ticket 'La Sinistra-l-Arcobaleno' with the Green Federation and the Party of Italian Communists.

voters set on holding the incumbents accountable for the plummeting economy would have been hard-pressed even to identify them.

The bottom-left panel traces electoral changes in Estonian parties. The early elections in Estonia were some of the most turbulent ones in all of Europe since 1990.[13] However, EIP steadily declined, falling to negligible levels in the most recent election. Between 2007 and 2011, EIP was zero: while the Estonian People's Union and the Estonian United Left formed a new joint list, it did not meet the 5 per cent inclusion threshold. Most CEE countries resemble the pattern of Estonia over time: while EIP was relatively high in the 1990s and early 2000s, in recent elections it has declined substantially.

The final panel traces EIP levels in Poland. The time series in Poland are interesting in that the early elections do not register high party change, yet EIP climbs gradually in subsequent elections, peaking at ten in 2001.[14] While Polish voters initially faced a high number of parties (111 in 1991 and 35 in 1993), relatively few of those meeting the 5 per cent threshold underwent electoral change. A decade later the picture was altogether different. Only one party that entered parliament in 2001, the Peasant Party, had not changed between 1997 and 2001. Law and Justice was a new party launched by the Kaczynski brothers

---

13. The comparatively high levels of party change found in the three Baltic countries agree with findings elsewhere (e.g., Bielasiak 2002; Jungerstam-Mulders 2006; Kreuzer and Pettai 2003).

14. The elections appear stable when looking at parties above the 5 per cent threshold. The EIP score does not reflect instability in smaller parties, however. Due to the scarcity of information on these parties in the media and in secondary sources, their coding is likely incomplete.

in 2001.[15] The League of Polish Families, soon to merge with the Movement for Reconstruction of Poland, was a splinter of Solidarity.[16] The Civic Platform had its roots in the Freedom Union and is coded here as a splinter.[17] Samoobrana, a very marginal party before 2001, received 10.2 per cent of the vote.[18] Finally, the party sweeping a plurality of votes was a newly formed joint list between the Democratic Left Alliance and the Union of Labour.[19] Following this turbulent election, EIP levels fell drastically in 2005 and again in 2007. Electoral instability in Polish parties was a fraction of 2001 levels in the most recent elections.[20]

More generally, EIP is higher in the post-socialist democracies (on average, EIP is 4.57 and 0.61 in CEE and WE, respectively); however, levels of EIP in some West European elections (e.g., Belgium and Iceland) are nearly as high as the figures in some East European elections (e.g., Hungary and the Czech Republic). Average EIP scores for the time period are highest in the Baltic countries, Bulgaria and Poland, closely followed by Italy. See Table A.2 in the Appendix for country profiles.

Robustness and validity

Aggregating party changes across elections raises several measurement issues: whether or not different types of party changes (e.g., mergers, splinters, disbanded parties) ought to be weighted equally; further, if party changes ought to be treated equally across parties of different size or weighted by electoral strength; and finally, how party change should be treated across party systems of varying sizes. I discuss each of these issues in turn and test the robustness of the EIP index to the coding protocol.

The EIP index weighs the six types of party changes equally as we do not have any *a priori* knowledge of the relative importance of each category. While each type of party change alters the menu of electoral alternatives presented to voters, some categories of instability arguably involve more drastic change in parties than others. The appearance of a new, unfamiliar party may be more drastic than, say, the reappearance of a familiar party upon leaving a joint list. However, as evinced

---

15. Law and Justice was not a splinter from the Centre Alliance which had disbanded when J. Kaczynski founded his new party.

16. League of Polish Families was founded by a group of legislators who dissented from the Solidarity parliamentary group in the Polish Sejm in September of 1998 (Katz & Koole 1999).

17. Civic Platform attracted many prominent national and local leaders of the Freedom Union, including its vice president Donald Tusk.

18. Samoobrana had appeared for election prior to 2001 and is not considered a new party.

19. This joint list is not part of the party-level data set because the latter party received only 4.7 per cent of the vote in 1997.

20. Between 2005 and 2007, EIP was two: the SRP-KPEiR joint list which received 11.4 per cent of the vote in 2005 disbanded by 2007 and a new joint list, LiD The Left and the Democrats, swept 13.15 per cent in 2007.

by the Italian case, changes in joint lists, mergers and splinters can completely transform electoral alternatives from election to election (*see* Table 3.1). Further, the relative importance of each category – e.g., should a splinter be given one or two thirds the weight of a new party? – is an empirical question that depends in part on our research question. Researchers are hence encouraged to test the effects of each types of party change on outcomes of interest. Chapters Four-Six illustrate this approach.

The second point that merits discussion is weighing party change by the electoral strength of parties. On one hand, treating change equally across parties may give undue weight to instability in small parties and thus overestimate the overall degree of instability between elections. On the other hand, the electoral strength of a party is not necessarily a good indicator of its importance in a party system; rather, the systemic role of a party determines the extent to which its appearance or disappearance affects electoral competition (see Mair 1989). Furthermore, a weighted index would confound change in parties with voter preferences by capturing the electoral share of transformed parties rather than change in and of itself. To avoid these problems while at the same time excluding marginal parties for which information was difficult to come by, the index adopts a 5 per cent inclusion threshold.[21] This threshold is at or above the electoral thresholds of most countries included in the dataset, thus only change in parliamentary parties is included. Change in small, marginal parties is excluded without relying on the electoral strength of each party.

Finally, levels of instability in part depend on the number of parties in a party system. EIP tends to be somewhat higher in party systems with more parties, though the relationship is far from deterministic.[22] Because EIP captures the entry and exit of parties from the system, it is interrelated with the total number of parties. As the two processes are not independent, standardising EIP by the number of parties would generate inequalities between elections of varying levels and types of EIP, and thus measurement bias.[23] As the index is not standardised by party system size, in subsequent chapters I control for the number of parties competing in an election.

The index was robust to the coding decisions described above. Varying the inclusion threshold to 3 per cent and 7 per cent produced a measure highly correlated with the EIP index (ρ=.97 and 0.95, respectively).[24] Furthermore, standardising the index by the total number of parties at election *t-1* or weighing party change by the vote share of each party or party list also produced a measure highly correlated

---

21. This is consistent with Janda (1980).

22. The number of parties at *t-1* and *t* is positively correlated with EIP (ρ =.49 and .42, respectively).

23. In the case of standardising by the total number of parties, EIP would always tend to be lower in party systems prone to the emergence of new parties, splinters and joint list exists (as the denominator, total number of parties, will be higher); the opposite would be true for party systems prone to the disbanding of parties, mergers and joint list entry.

24. The correlations are equally strong for WE and CEE, respectively (ρ=.94 and 0.96 with the 3 per cent threshold; and 0.91 and 0.85 for the 7 per cent threshold, respectively).

Figure 3.3: Scatter plots of EIP and electoral volatility by region

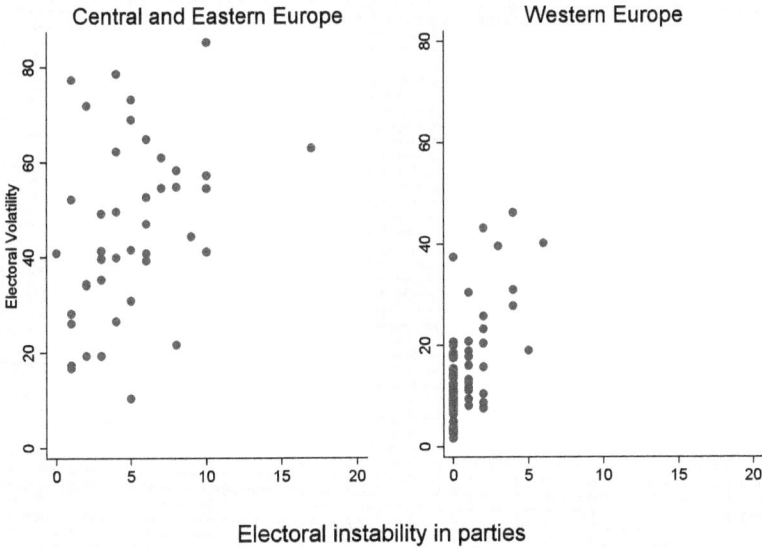

Source for data on electoral volatility: Powell & Tucker (2013)

with EIP (ρ=0.91 and ρ=.89, respectively). I also test how diffuse party change is in the system. The larger the value of EIP, the greater the per centage of parties changing between elections (ρ = 0.76), suggesting that high EIP is generally not concentrated in a small cluster of parties.

Finally, I examine the external validity of EIP by comparing it to related indices. First, Figure 3.3 plots the relationship between EIP and electoral volatility in the new and mature European democracies, respectively.[25] Because party changes are reflected in volatility scores, the relationship is largely tautological. Although we cannot speak of the direction of causality between EIP and volatility, the general trends across the two regions largely conform to prior expectations. While in the East high party change and volatility go hand in hand, in Western Europe vote swings among stable parties are the norm. In the latter, ninety-five per cent of elections have an EIP score of five or less while volatility in those same elections is on average thirteen, and as high as forty-three per cent. These trends are as we might expect from the previous literature establishing that voters are the destabilising force in West European electoral politics (Inglehart 1977; Mair *et al.* 2004; Rose and Urwin 1970) while electoral swings in CEE are associated with change in parties (Powell and Tucker 2014; Rose and Munro 2009; Tavits 2008). Further strengthening the construct validity of the index is the strong correlation between EIP and Powell and Tucker's Type A Volatility that captures the segment

---

25.   Data on electoral volatility comes from Powell and Tucker (2014).

of volatility due to party entry and exit (.38 and .70 in CEE and WE, respectively) and the low correlation between EIP and Type B Volatility that reflects volatility among stable parties (.1 and .01).

Conclusions

The study of party system instability has gained importance in recent years. The frequency of party changes in modern democracies has stimulated a number of recent articles and books exploring the dynamics of instability in party organisations (e.g., Mair *et al.* 2004; Sikk 2005; Sikk 2012; Tavits 2006; Tavits 2008). To facilitate the study of electoral instability in parties, the European Consortium of Political Research held a section titled 'Rethinking Intra-Party Cohesion in Time of Party Transformation' for its 2017 Joint Sessions. This recent scholarship indicates that political scientists have identified an important phenomenon which has not yet been adequately measured.

This chapter was driven by the recognition that currently used indicators often conflate the roles of political elites and masses in destabilising party systems, or are partial and limited to a handful of cases, thus limiting cross-national comparability. In addition to supplying detailed, qualitative data on party transformations in twenty-seven European democracies, this chapter proposes an indicator of electoral instability in parties that is comparable cross-nationally and that considerably reduces endogeneity between voter choice and party change. The election-level indicator is robust to the coding protocol adopted in this chapter and has good construct validity when compared to available related indicators.

As will be illustrated in the chapters that follow, one fruitful venue for future research that these data make possible is the understanding of the interplay between voters and parties. Extant accounts of voter behaviour are usually static, as parties are merely the recipients of voter evaluations under fixed institutional settings. The present chapter affords parties the agency to influence voter knowledge of party positions, and by extension voter choice. It thus conceives of elections in fairly realistic terms – as dynamic, give-and-take processes between voters and parties.

Beyond this book, the data on party instability will allow future research to disentangle the effects of party change on how voters decide, thus closing an important theoretical gap in the interaction between political elites and voters. The data should also be useful in comparative research on party and electoral systems. Given the importance of party system stabilisation for democratic consolidation, the index will enable researchers to study the incentive structures of elites in triggering instability.[26]

---

26. While some research exists on the incentives of new parties to emerge (e.g., Sikk 2005; Sikk 2012; Tavits 2006), the origins of other organisational changes in parties are not well understood.

Chapter Four

Seeking Information: Voter Knowledge of Party Positions

Representative democracy is based on the delegation of power, and so voters ought to have sufficient knowledge of competing parties to cast a meaningful ballot.[1] In this chapter I develop testable hypotheses on the linkages between the stability of electoral spaces and voter knowledge thereof. I seek answers to the following question: Can elections imbued with high party instability be characterised as 'low-information' environments? Following from the theoretical framework developed in Chapter Two, I contend that party instability obstructs the facilitating functions of parties for how voters decide, with negative consequences for voter familiarity with the parties up for election.

In thinking specifically about political knowledge, I extend on the theoretical discussion in Chapter Two in several ways. I consider how the impact of party instability may depend on both its type and overall degree as well as on voters' disparate abilities to handle electoral complexity. I find that while voters tend to be less familiar with the positions of brand new parties, for example, other types of party transformations (such as new mergers and joint lists) help consolidate and clarify preexisting parties' positions. I argue further that voters are generally less knowledgeable of electoral alternatives when many party transformations take place in an election. Due to the demands placed on their attention and cognition, voters are generally less capable of taking party cues in erratic elections. I find that this relationship is conditional on voters' educational backgrounds. As overall instability increases, the positive effect of education on political knowledge diminishes, suggesting that even the well-educated have difficulty sorting through electoral alternatives as parties change. Finally, the negative effects of instability are direr in established democracies that experience only occasional party changes. This may well hint at a learning effect where citizens who experience a frequent transformation of parties become accustomed to instability and adapt more readily. I conclude by discussing the implications of these results for present theories of political knowledge.

Political knowledge under unstable parties

As I have argued in Chapter Two, parties are not always able to organise and communicate political alternatives. Some party systems provide voters with a

---

1. The focus here is not on knowledge of current events or civics facts but on knowledge of the ideological positions of parties competing for election.

set of electoral alternatives that are relatively stable across time. Through their cohesion and stability, parties simplify a relatively complex political reality and facilitate voters' familiarity with policy alternatives. However, in many democracies, parties change so erratically, that they add more confusion than orderliness to the political landscape. In such elections, the difficulty of finding accurate information may unreasonably raise the costs of becoming informed. Paul Sniderman (2000, p.84-85) argues that in a 'chaotic' political order, electoral alternatives are obscure and complex, and as a result voters have difficulty making sense of the electoral menu. Do parties in less consolidated party systems equally facilitate the acquisition of political information and, by extension, the electoral calculus of voters? The following sections turn to instability in political parties as a potentially consequential phenomenon for electoral information seeking.

What are the implications of party instability for voters' familiarity with electoral alternatives? The answer to this question likely depends both on the type and the sheer quantity of party change in a given election. Take new and splinter parties, first. We can reasonably expect that voters be less familiar with both brand new parties and parties that have formed after splitting from preexisting parties than they are with parties that have competed in previous elections (Expectation 1A). An important caveat, however, is that in a small number of elections in Central and Eastern Europe (CEE), genuinely new parties have been so successful that Sikk (2012) has argued that 'newness' is an electorally advantageous strategy. Because of sheer newness, in some cases parties receive substantial press coverage, potentially leading voters to become familiar with their platforms and elect them into office. Consequently, voters in CEE may be more familiar with the general ideological leanings of brand new parties (Expectation 1B).

Another common source of electoral instability in parties is the formation of mergers and joint lists. Such changes may be difficult for voters to track and comprehend because, first, voters may not become aware of such changes as they are not readily observable on the electoral menu; and second, when voters become aware of changes, they must update their associations of the new party formations and their policy positions – a task that requires additional cognitive effort. Observers of Italian elections can attest that such instability is complex. Compare the list of party alternatives in the 2006 and 2008 Italian elections (Table 3.1 in Chapter Three). While not a single party was either new or had disbanded between 2006 and 2008, the party offerings look considerably different. On the whole, becoming informed of changing electoral alternatives requires more attention and greater cognitive effort from voters, and thus we can reasonably expect that voters are less familiar with transformed parties' platforms than with the positions of unaltered parties (Expectation 2A).

Despite the complexity of joint list transformations, it is also conceivable that such changes in fact simplify voters' cognitive task. New party mergers and joint lists may help consolidate and clarify the resulting parties' ideological positions. Arguably such was the case in the Czech Civic Democratic Party's split from the Civic Forum, as the former advocated neoliberal economic reforms not endorsed by the latter (see Roberts 2009). Voters may be equally or more familiar with the ideological leanings of parties that have merged together or grouped into new joint lists than with the positions of stable parties (Expectation 2B). The clarifying function of such changes, however, may be masked by their sheer quantity in a given election. I turn to this point next.

Apart from the types of changes parties undergo, the overall levels of instability in any given election may have an impact on voters' familiarity with the electoral menu, regardless of the type of party change. In elections where many parties transform at once, the task of identifying parties and their respective positions requires more cognitive effort and attention. As multiple changes in political parties put greater demands on voters' attention, voters embedded in elections of high instability are less likely to take cuing information from parties than are voters in elections with stable parties (Expectation 3).[2]

Furthermore, voters are not equally prepared to process complex electoral information, potentially resulting in unequal effects of party instability on political knowledge for different groups of voters. Higher educational attainment is indicative of citizens' ability to deal with abstract information and also of their interest in politics (Campbell *et al.* 1960; Converse 1964). Due to greater cognitive capacity and higher political interest, well-educated voters are likely better equipped to muddle through a menu of erratic parties. As elections of high party instability place higher cognitive demands on voters, the educated will continue to enjoy an advantage or, in being better equipped to deal with a complex electoral context, may augment their advantage. If inequalities in political knowledge are due to cognitive differences alone, then more cognitively taxing electoral contexts should maintain or reinforce the gap between voters of different educational attainment (Expectation 4A).

However, if political parties facilitate the acquisition of information in sending party cues, then increasing levels of instability will weaken the positive relationship between education and political knowledge (Expectation 4B). The argument is as follows: When unstable parties do not send clear signals, they cannot facilitate the identification of electoral alternatives or the use of heuristics, such as party ideology. Better educated voters rely on heuristics at higher rates than do voters of low educational backgrounds (Lau and Redlawsk 2001). As a result, the better educated may be more adversely affected when electoral alternatives do not easily lend themselves to the use of heuristics. If that is the case, differences in political knowledge among voters of varying educational levels will gradually subside with high degrees of instability, with information-rich voters losing more than their information-poor counterparts.

The final set of expectations assesses the effect of party instability on preexisting political inequalities among voters. As Downs (1957, 223) puts it, 'systematic variations in [the] amount of free information received and ability to assimilate

---

2. We may further postulate a nonlinear relationship. In an election in which only a few parties change, voters may be capable of identifying new and transformed parties and gleaning their positions. However, if multiple parties transform repeatedly, voters are less likely to keep track of electoral alternatives. However, the analyses below did not uncover robust nonlinear effects.

may strongly influence the distribution of political power in a democracy.' The educated already exert greater influence on public policy by turning out at higher rates and by expressing better their preferences in the vote (e.g., Andersen *et al.* 2005; Delli Carpini and Keeter 1996, 256–8; Gomez and Wilson 2001; Lau and Redlawsk 2001; Marquis 2010; Sniderman *et al.* 1990). Expectation 4A postulates that party instability may serve to increase further the preexisting gap between voters of differing educational backgrounds. In contrast, support for Expectation 4B would imply that high levels of party instability have an equalising effect; the knowledge gap between voters of different educational backgrounds will gradually subside as parties cease to facilitate the identification of electoral alternatives. Testing these final expectations will further our understanding of the distribution of power in electoral democracy and the impact political parties exert thereon.

Data and method of analysis

The expectations have empirical implications for cross-sectional time-series tests. I use survey data from fifty-four elections of twenty-five European countries[3], 1996–2011, by appending the first three modules of the Comparative Study of Electoral Systems (CSES). To estimate the dependent variable, knowledge of parties' ideological leanings, I use survey questions available in the CSES. I calculate how much each respondent's placement of each party on a 0 to 10 left-right ideological scale deviates from political experts' placement of the corresponding parties on the same scale.[4] Larger values indicate higher inaccuracy in respondents' political knowledge; for ease of interpretation, I reverse the scale.

I operationalise party instability with six categories of electoral change in parties, as described in Chapter Three. For this set of fifty-four elections, the average EIP score was 1.4, and roughly half of the elections in the sample experience some party instability.[5] Figure 4.1 displays the per cent of parties affected by each type of change in Central and Eastern and in Western Europe, respectively. Party change is present in a large per centage of CEE elections and in a non-negligible per cent of WE ones. Mergers, splinters and changes in joint lists are prevalent in the East while only four per cent of parties that pass the 5 per cent threshold can be classified as new in the West. In the latter, party change is considerably less common and affects between one and three per cent of all parties.

---

3. See Table A.4 in the Appendix for a list of election studies. The data collected on instability in parties is described in Chapter Three.

4. In one Estonia-2011, CSES expert placements of parties were hugely off from both the average placement by voters and an independent expert survey (Vowles, Hellwig and Coffey 2009). For example, the conservative Union Pro Patria and Res Publica was placed on the extreme left by CSES experts while both voters and the experts in Vowles *et al.* correctly placed the parties to the right. For this election, I have used the Vowles *et al.* placements rounded to the nearest digit. See the Appendix for more information.

5. The mean EIP scores per country are listed in Table A.4 in the Appendix.

Figure 4.1: Per cent of parties changing by region (CSES elections)

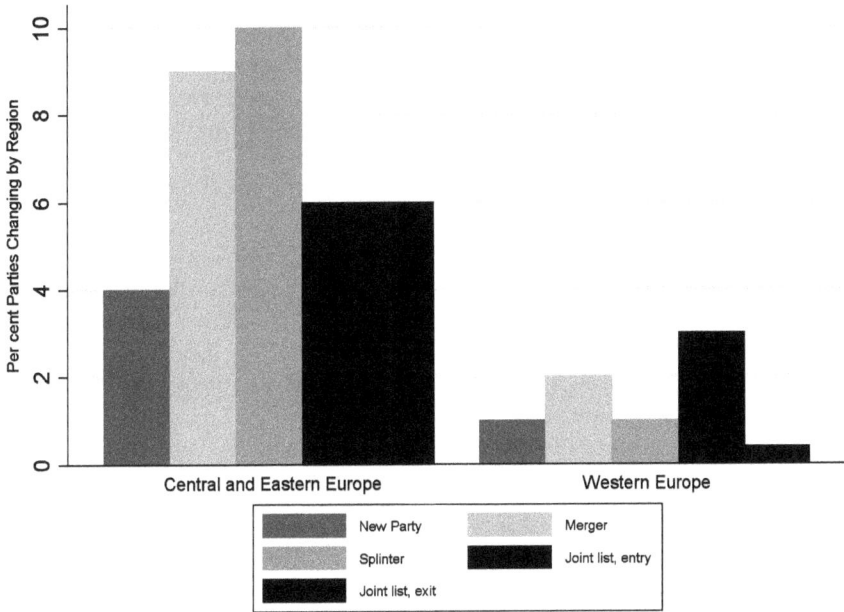

Control variables

The act of becoming politically informed implies opportunity and transaction costs. Some individual characteristics lower the costs of acquiring information while certain institutional features increase the availability of information and thus lower its cost (Berggren 2001; Delli Carpini and Keeter 1996; Fraile 2014). In addition to education, gender and age, I control for ideological distance from each party as voters may be more familiar with parties in their corner of the ideological spectrum. In multiparty systems the availability of information is greater due to the incentives of political elites to differentiate themselves from competitors (Berggren 2001, Gordon and Segura 1997). I control for the effective number of electoral parties (ENEP) because in party systems with a very high number of political parties information is more costly to individuals (Laakso and Taagepera 1979). The competitiveness of electoral systems has been found to motivate voters to stay politically informed. Hence, I control for district magnitude and dummy variables for proportional and majoritarian electoral system rules (Gordon and Segura 1997). Furthermore, bicameral legislatures increase the complexity between vote choice and electoral outcomes and may thus create a disincentive for citizens to gather information (bicameral=1). The frequency of elections may increase the salience of party platforms, and hence the less time (in months) that has elapsed since the previous national election, the more informed voters should be. If the information to cast a meaningful vote is not useful to translate the vote into a seat, then the individual will have no incentives to be fully involved in the electoral process. Seat-vote disparity is estimated as the average vote-seat share deviation of the two largest parties in the polity (Lijphart 1984).[6] Finally, Cook's Distance tests revealed that three elections had high leverage and/or influence: Italy, Bulgaria and Poland-2001. Following previous studies (e.g., Anderson and Beramendi 2012; Remmer 1991; Singer 2013), I include binary variables for each outlier elections.[7]

Method of analysis

The dependent variable is the familiarity of each individual with each party in a given election, and hence each individual appears as many times in the dataset as the number of parties she placed on the left-right scale. The data is stacked at the individual per party level and contains repeated observations on the individual. I take account of nested data structure by fitting multilevel models clustered by individual and by election. To test expectations 1A-B and 2A-B, I include the five types of party instability as independent variables at the party-level of analysis.[8] In addition, I test for a main effect of EIP: $K_{ijk} = \beta_0 + \beta_1 EIP_k + \gamma X_{ijk} + \zeta_{jk} + \zeta_k + \varepsilon_{ijk}$ (1), where K_{ijk} is individual *j*'s knowledge of party *i*'s left-right position in election *k*; EIP_k is overall level of party instability in election *k*; X_{ijk} is a vector of covariates and γ a vector of slopes for X_{ijk}; ζ_{jk} is the random intercept for individual *j* and election *k*; ζ_k is the random intercept for election *k*. A negative sign on β1 in equation (1) would offer support for Expectation 3. Finally, I operationalise the marginal effect of EIP on education with an interaction term between EIP_k and education: $K_{ijk} = \beta_0 + \beta_1 EIP_k + \beta_2 EIP_k * Education + \gamma X_{ijk} + \zeta_{jk} + \zeta_k + \varepsilon_{ijk}$ (2). A negative sign on β2 can be taken as evidence that increasing levels of instability weaken the positive effect of education on political knowledge.

Empirical findings

The analyses offer empirical support for the overall negative effect of party instability on political knowledge. This is the case for new parties, splinter parties and parties that leave joint lists from one election to the next. However, voters are more familiar with parties that merge or enter a joint list with one or more other parties. The sheer quantity of instability is also important. The higher party instability is, the lower levels of political knowledge. The magnitude of

---

6. Figures on seat-vote disparity are based on own estimates with the CSES data. The remaining individual and contextual variables come from the CSES.

7. Cook's D revealed that Bulgaria and Italy were influential outliers while Poland had an extreme value on EIP but was not an influential outlier. See Appendix to Chapter Four for a full analysis of outliers. I discuss the substantive reasons behind these outliers below as well as their potential contribution to theory building.

8. Note that it is not possible to measure the effect of disbanded parties at the party level because respondents were not asked to place these parties.

Figure 4.2: Political knowledge by electoral instability in parties: residuals from the null model of political knowledge

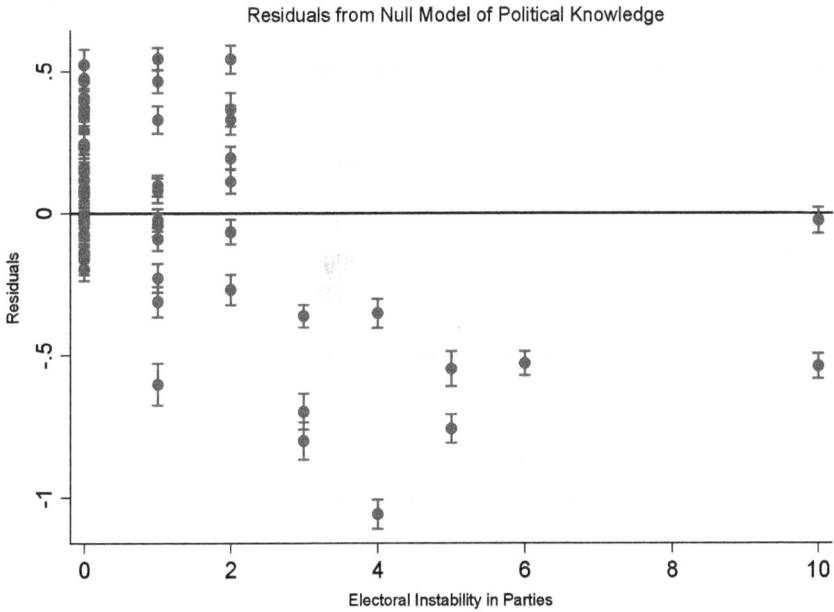

Residuals from Null Model of Political Knowledge

Note: The outliers at EIP value of 10 are Bulgaria-2001 and Poland-2001. Italy-2006 has a residual value below -1 and an EIP score of 4.

these relationships also varies across new and established democracies, being considerably greater in the latter. Finally, with increasing instability, the predictive power of education gradually subsides. Differences in political knowledge between voters of differing educational backgrounds decline as instability rises. The results are discussed in greater detail below.

A baseline model of political knowledge without any predictors indicates that the overall mean across elections is high with a relatively small between-election variance (mean=8.27, with predicted election mean ranging from 8.17 to 8.37). A comparison between the model with individual-level predictors and the model with individual predictors and party instability variables indicated that the latter help explain roughly twelve per cent of the between-election variance in political knowledge.[9] Based on the null model, Figure 4.2 displays the residuals of political knowledge mapped onto election-level EIP. Most elections are clustered at low levels of instability. Mean levels of knowledge become lower as instability

---

9.   The election-level variance in the baseline models with individual-level predictors is 0.1409; it shrinks to 0.1237, or by roughly twelve per cent, when party- and election-level instability variables are added as covariates. See the Appendix for full model results.

increases. The time-series data on Poland can help illustrate the trend. In 2007 Poland experienced a relatively stable election (EIP=2) and registered about average political knowledge as compared to the sample. When instability had been slightly higher in 2005 (EIP=3), the Polish were on average misplacing each party by one third of a point more than they did in the 2007 election. When EIP was high in 1997, the Polish misplaced each party by half a point more than in 2007.

Next I examine the effects of individual-, party- and election-level covariates. The model results in Table 4.1 include five binary variables indicating whether or not a party is new, splinter, has merged, or entered or exited a joint list. The analyses reveal distinct effects of the different types of party change on political knowledge. In most types of party change, instability results in loss of knowledge. On average voters misplace new parties by 0.4 points more than they do preexisting parties. Voters are also less knowledgeable about parties that have abandoned joint lists, misplacing them by 0.6 points compared to stable parties. The effect for splinter parties is smaller in magnitude but also statistically significant and robust. Two categories of change – parties that have either merged or entered a joint list with one or more other parties – exert a modest positive effect on knowledge. Voters are better able to place such parties by 0.2 points on average. These findings lend support to the argument that new mergers and joint lists serve to consolidate party positions, thus clarifying their ideological stance to voters.[10]

Next, we test the effect of overall levels of instability on political knowledge and its interaction with education. Coefficients and standard errors of the model testing Expectation 3 are presented in Table 4.1, Model 1. The coefficient on party instability is negative and statistically significant. Its magnitude can be compared to that of having university education; any three changes on the electoral menu are roughly equivalent in magnitude to the inverse effect of education. University education has a strong and positive impact on voters' correct placement of party positions. A voter without a university degree is likely to be off by a third of a point in placing a party on the eleven-point scale. Model 2 tests the marginal effect of party instability on education and uncovers a negative effect ($p<0.01$; see Fig. 3) consistent with Expectation 4B. With increasing values of EIP, the explanatory power of education gradually subsides; from zero to eight party changes, the advantage of the well-educated decreases by a third. While education maintains a positive effect on knowledge for all values of EIP, this evidence implies that the stability of party alternatives facilitates the acquisition of electoral information and by extension the use of party ideology as a voting heuristic.

The rich qualitative data on party instability allows us also to explore the impact of party instability on voters' knowledge across new and developed democracies, respectively. I include a set of interaction terms between a binary variable for Western Europe and each category of party instability (Model 3). In nearly all cases, the interaction term is negative, hinting at the fact that the same types of

---

10. It is also plausible that voters place such parties more accurately because they receive more media attention than do preexisting parties that remain unchanged. The data does not allow us to weigh in on these arguments.

Table 4.1: Knowledge of party positions

	(1)	(2)	(3)
Party Instability			
New party	−0.409***	−0.409***	0.106***
	0.0172	0.0172	0.0287
Merged	0.203***	0.203***	0.398***
	0.0142	0.0142	0.0200
JL Entry	0.167***	0.167***	0.334***
	0.0173	0.0173	0.0243
Splinter	−0.119***	−0.119***	−0.065**
	0.0157	0.0157	0.0241
JL Exit	−0.630***	−0.630***	−0.534***
	0.0273	0.0273	0.0288
EIP	−0.088**	−0.086*	−0.120*
	0.0338	0.0338	0.0493
Education			
University education	0.297***	0.295***	0.297***
	0.0085	0.0085	0.0085
EIP * University education		−0.012**	
		0.0044	
Region			
W. Europe			0.094
			0.1384
New party * W. Europe			−0.829***
			0.0360
Merged * W. Europe			−0.424***
			0.0284
JL Entry * W. Europe			−0.219***
			0.0362
Splinter * W. Europe			−0.020
			0.0327
EIP * W. Europe			0.184*
			0.0894
Control Variables			
Age	0.004***	0.004***	0.004***
	0.0010	0.0010	0.0010
Age * Age	−0.000***	−0.000***	−0.000***
	0.0000	0.0000	0.0000

(Continued)

Table 4.1 *(continued)*

	(1)	(2)	(3)
Male	0.119***	0.119***	0.119***
	0.0063	0.0063	0.0063
Party age	0.000***	0.000***	0.000***
	0.0001	0.0001	0.0001
Distance from party	−0.071***	−0.071***	−0.071***
	0.0012	0.0012	0.0012
ENEP, log	−0.311	−0.312	−0.206
	0.2125	0.2124	0.2071
MDM	0.001	0.001	0.000
	0.0010	0.0010	0.0010
Proportional	0.162	0.162	0.249*
	0.1207	0.1206	0.1186
Majoritarian	0.158	0.159	0.109
	0.2013	0.2012	0.2096
Bicameral legislature	−0.104	−0.103	−0.061
	0.0798	0.0798	0.0775
Months since last election	0.005	0.005	0.004
	0.0046	0.0046	0.0043
Compulsory voting	−0.162	−0.162	−0.534
	0.2953	0.2952	0.3148
Seat-vote disparity	−0.033*	−0.033*	−0.017
	0.0162	0.0162	0.0169
Italy - 2006	−0.933***	−0.935***	−1.576***
	0.2826	0.2825	0.3627
Bulgaria - 2001	1.144**	1.139**	1.224**
	0.4126	0.4124	0.4748
Poland - 2001	0.450	0.447	0.684
	0.3776	0.3774	0.4365
Constant	8.693***	8.580***	8.338***
	0.3605	0.3806	0.3748
Variance components			
Intercept (respondent)	0.0640	0.0640	0.3699
	0.0125	0.0125	0.0039
Intercept (election	0.3690	0.3690	0.0577
	0.0039	0.0039	0.0113
N	390,387	390,387	390,387

Note: Coefficients and standard errors from a three-level model of political knowledge are reported. The sample contains 390,387 respondent-party pairs from 74,038 respondents in 54 elections. Coefficient estimates are maximum likelihood unstandardised coefficients. Analyses were performed in Stata 12 with the .xtmixed command. *$p < 0.05$, **$p < 0.01$, ***$p < 0.001$

instability have more severe consequences for political knowledge in established democracies. Take the emergence of new party formations as an example. Voters in the post-communist democracies tend to be slightly *more* familiar with the positions of newcomers than they are with those of pre-existing parties. This stands in sharp contrast to Western Europe where nearly all types of party change exert a strong negative effect and the impact of newcomers is largest in magnitude (a loss of 0.72 points compared to stable parties). Similarly for mergers, while voters in WE tend to know less about the positions of new mergers (–0.26), the latter contribute to gains in political knowledge in CEE (0.398). Indeed Sikk's (2005) findings of 'newness' as an electoral strategy in CEE may also help explain why party change often contributes to political knowledge in the region. The implications of these results are discussed in the concluding section.

Discussion of outliers: Italy, Bulgaria and Poland

Given the model fit, three elections stood out as outliers: Italy-2006, Bulgaria-2001 and Poland-2001. Italy had lower-than-expected levels of political knowledge while voters in both Bulgaria and Poland were far more familiar with parties than the model predicted. Each of the three cases presented special circumstances, including major electoral reform and party system realignment. The preliminary

Figure 4.3: Marginal effect of electoral instability in parties on education (estimates based on Table 1, Model 2)

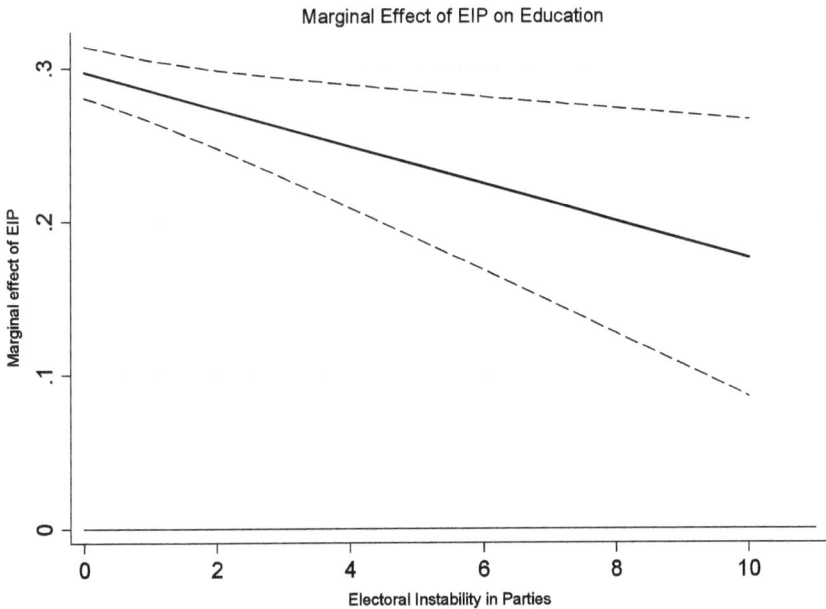

Marginal Effect of EIP on Education

conclusions drawn here may aid in theory building and in guiding future empirical research on political knowledge.

In 2006, Italy registered lower-than-expected levels of familiarity with political parties. What stands out about the 2006 elections in Italy is the sweeping electoral reform instituted by Berlusconi's coalition – and the party instability it triggered – in the year prior to the elections. The goal of the reform was to stabilise the party system by incentivising the creation of large party coalitions and reducing the influence of small parties in parliament (Baldini 2011). The newly instituted electoral thresholds stimulated parties to compete under pre-electoral coalitions, a kind of party change that is not common across European democracies and was not accounted for in the measure of party change used in this book.[11] While a few parties appeared and transformed before 2006, changes stemming in electoral coalitions (which themselves appear and disappear) were much more prevalent.[12]

Since the electoral reform of 2005, changes in preelectoral coalitions are an integral part of the Italian party system and may help account for the lower-than-expected levels of political knowledge. Consistent with Expectation 2A, one possible interpretation of the results is that Italian voters were overall less knowledgeable of party positions due to the additional changes in pre-electoral alliances not accounted for by the EIP measure. In other words, the measure of party instability underestimated real levels of party change in Italy. In the case of larger party groupings, as in pre-electoral coalitions in Italy, it is likely that the ideological differences between parties are larger, thus increasing the chances of voters misplacing individual parties. A second possible explanation for the mismatch between party change and knowledge lies in the Italian party system where voters focus on party groupings rather than individual parties. The party-centred survey items in the CSES may consequently be a poor fit for the Italian context and may simply underestimate actual levels of electoral knowledge. While the present analysis cannot rule between these competing explanations, future work should investigate the unusually low levels of knowledge in Italian elections and their possible causes.[13]

Unlike Italian voters, Bulgarian and Polish voters in 2011 were far more familiar with party positions than the model predicted. Both elections were unusual in the great number of party changes since the previous elections. However, this did not generate a high drop in political knowledge, as the model would predict. The

---

11. Preelectoral coalitions exist in other countries, including Belgium and France. Italian preelectoral coalitions stand out in the great number of changes they often experience between elections.

12. In 2006, parties competed under the umbrellas of the Union (L'Unione) or the House of Freedoms (Casa delle Liberta). Shortly before the elections, the existing (L'Ulivo) was replaced by the Union. The new coalition absorbed parties that were previously not members of L'Ulivo, including the Communist Refoundation Party.

13. A third possible explanation is the unaccounted role of the mass media in electoral campaigns. The characteristics of mass media have been shown shape citizens' levels of information. Independent media are generally associated with higher levels of political knowledge (Leeson 2008; Schoonvelde 2014). The Italian media system is notorious for its fragmentation, polarisation and limited political independence (Mancini 2013). Italy's Freedom House ratings on media freedom are comparable to those of some CEE countries during the transition years. As the lack of media

unique circumstances in each set of elections may help us understand their deviation from the pattern. Take the Bulgarian elections first. The deposed monarch Simeon II returned to Bulgaria where he formed NDSV (National Movement Simeon II) just months prior to the elections. Existing parties squabbled during NDSV's rise in popularity and arguably initiated changes in response to the electoral threat NDSV represented. The elections were exceptional, not only in the high number of party changes, but also in the interest the electoral campaign generated among citizens and in the media. The 'return of the king' appealed to patriotic sentiments, as evinced by elevated turnout, and citizens felt enthusiastic about the upcoming elections.[14]

The 2001 elections in Poland had many parallels to the Bulgarian ones. Polish voters, too, saw high party turnover. The elections have been described as 'a seismic shift' and 'an earthquake in Polish politics' because they led to a major restructuring of the party system: 'The election marked the end of the historic division between the heirs of communism and the heirs of Solidarity' (Millard 2003). While the Solidarity coalition failed for the first time to obtain representation in the Sejm, the elections saw the rise of a number of populist parties: Self-Defence, PiS (Law and Justice) and LPR (League of Polish Families) which between them gained over 25 per cent of the vote. The rise of populist parties and the accompanying scandals saw heightened media attention to the new parties and the elections in general.[15]

Notwithstanding the unique circumstances in each set of elections, the two outliers tell a similar story in terms of the effects of high party instability on political knowledge. When instability is particularly elevated, the media tend to pay greater attention to the electoral campaign, and this in turn helps offset the knowledge costs of high party turnover. The cross-regional analyses in Model 3 also hint at this; voters who experience only occasional peaks in party change (e.g., Western Europe) are penalised more harshly than voters in fluid party systems (e.g., CEE). Too few elections in the current study reach levels of EIP which allow for a systematic evaluation of this hypothesis. The cases of Bulgaria and Poland nevertheless emphasise the important role of the media in fostering awareness about party positions and in possibly offsetting the ill-effects of instability through intense elections coverage. These insights, along with the insights gleaned from the case of Italy, can help motivate future directions of research in this area.

---

freedom overlaps geographically with high levels of party instability, I control for media freedom and rerun all models (See Table A.6 in the Appendix). The results described above are robust to this model specification. Note that the interaction between EIP and region is no longer significant, suggesting that media freedom may hold the power in explaining differences in information acquisition across young and mature democracies.

14. Turnout was eight to eleven per cent higher in 2001 than in the preceding and following elections.

15. The financial scandals related to the leaders of one of the new parties, the PiS, and were aired as documentaries during prime viewing time before the election. The campaign was also fueled by populist rhetoric about a more severe penal code and full disclosure of politicians' private assets, two matters that also received plenty of media coverage prior to the election. Another new party, the LPR, benefited from coverage in a Catholic nationalist media outlet, Radio Marija. See Szczerbiak (2002).

Conclusions

This chapter has explored the relationship between the stability of electoral alternatives and voters' familiarity with competing parties' general ideological orientations. The main finding, that voters tend to be less knowledgeable of party positions as parties transform between elections, is conditional on both the type of party change and on voters' levels of education. While voters tend to be less familiar with the positions of brand new parties and splinter parties, new mergers and joint lists arguably help consolidate and clarify preexisting parties' positions and result in higher levels of knowledge among voters. Further as overall levels of instability increase, the positive effect of education on political knowledge diminishes. The negative marginal effect of party instability on education suggests that even the well-educated have difficulty sorting through electoral alternatives as parties change. In answering the question posed at the beginning of this chapter, elections characterised by party instability can be considered low-information environments. These findings have important theoretical implications as they advance our understanding of the role parties play in the acquisition of electoral information.

On one hand, the findings of this chapter put a question mark over the suitability of complex information environments to a representative democracy in which voters turn out to be well informed about the political parties competing in elections. Electoral complexity has a negative impact on voters' familiarity with parties as voters are susceptible to even modest levels of party change. The advantage of the well-educated voters who most often rely on party ideology as a heuristic shrinks drastically in elections of high party change. Based on past research linking political knowledge to turnout and reasoned vote choice, high party instability thus spells bad news for electoral representation. On the other hand, and as I argue in the chapter to follow, low levels of familiarity with party positions do not preclude ideological voting. Instead, those voters embedded in erratic elections are more likely to rely on the direction and intensity of parties' ideological appeals rather than their exact positions in policy space. Lower levels of knowledge do not translate into a lack of programmatic voting; rather, they shift the ways in which voters piece together party positions and use ideology appeals.

It is important to recognise that party instability can also bode well for political representation. After all, new parties may form in response to issues and/or constituencies that are poorly represented by existing parties (e.g., Harmel and Robertson 1985; Müller-Rommel 2002). Recent studies have questioned this long-held assumption, however, evincing instead that parties often form and transform without addressing new political grievances or representing previously neglected constituencies (Sikk 2012). Rather, elites resolve conflicts by creating new parties with weak ideological platforms (Tavits 2008). While this chapter does not weigh in on this debate directly, it points out that, apart from the ideological stances taken by parties, the sheer act of transformation is consequential for political behaviour and electoral representation.

Furthermore, the analyses in this chapter uncover interesting cross-regional variation in how instability affects voters' knowledge of party alternatives. Perhaps contrary to expectations, it is not voters in less consolidated party systems that are most adversely affected but rather voters in stable party systems that experience only occasional instability. Frequent changes in parties may condition voters in the former to adapt to a relatively complex political reality by staying alert to party transformations. Conversely, occasional peaks in party instability do not seem to prepare voters in established democracies equally well to sort through transforming parties. It is plausible that voters in Western Europe do not become informed of changed party positions because the media do not take such parties seriously and hence do not give them due coverage. In contrast, the media may be more receptive to the high number of electorally competitive parties undergoing transformation in CEE elections (*see* Fig. 1), thus giving substantial coverage to their campaigns. While the present chapter cannot weigh in on these competing explanations, the data on party instability can be used to address such questions in future research.

Voter knowledge of party alternatives has important implications for overall electoral decision-making; it is essential if voters are to elect candidates who represent their interests in policy-making. Informed citizens make better electoral choices: they turn out at elections and vote consistently with their own issue preferences and performance evaluations. The stability of party alternatives is therefore likely to have further implications for voter decision-making, beyond knowledge of party positions. The following two chapters explore how voters make decisions as the electoral ground beneath them shifts.

Chapter Five

Heuristics for Unstable Parties: How Voters Cope

The previous chapter explored the implications of party instability for voters' familiarity with party positions. Overall, voters were shown to be *less* familiar with party positions when parties transform, with important caveats for the type of party transformation taking place and voters' own levels of political sophistication. The present chapter continues to probe the consequences of party instability for electoral decision-making. A number of influential theories have shaped our understanding of how voters decide between electoral alternatives, but we have no real sense of the extent to which these theories apply when the electoral choice set is fluid. How do voters cope in complex elections with new information that is not effectively communicated to them?

Here I re-examine the decision-making rules that govern voters' choices when parties are unstable. One of the questions this chapter addresses is the extent to which standard theories of voting continue to hold for decision-making in complex electoral environments. That is, when the alternatives in an election are fluid, do voters rely on the same set of heuristics as when the choice set is fixed and well defined? I attempt to parse out further the kinds of coping mechanisms voters develop in order to adapt in complex information environments. One surprising finding in Chapter Four was that party instability has a more negative effect on political knowledge in contexts where it occurs only occasionally. Hence, it is plausible that voters learn to adapt to high levels of party instability by using a different set of decision-making rules that require lower levels of information.[1] In particular, I focus here on three heuristics that may help voters decide in low-information elections: ideology, the personal vote and instability itself.

First and foremost, the chief heuristic that has been used to understand vote choice is political ideology (Popkin 1991; Sniderman, Brody and Tetlock 1991; Lau and Redlawsk 2001, 2006). Where voters can identify a party as being left or right of centre, they can infer its positions on a number of policy issues; ideology thus serves as an informational shortcut. I re-examine if and *how* voters use political ideology when the choice set of parties is non-fixed (Downs 1957; Rabinowitz and MacDonald 1989). While we might expect that voters are simply less likely to vote on left-right ideology considerations, I argue instead that voters *will* take into account party positions but will do so in different ways for parties that are new and for those that are stable. While standard theories of proximity voting

---

1.   Alvarez (1998) shows that voters are more strongly influenced by factors unrelated to policy when they cannot distinguish parties' policy positions.

require voters to pinpoint party positions exactly (Downs 1954), low-information models of vote choice entail considerably less information about party positions (Rabinowitz and MacDonald 1989). In the latter model, voters need to discern the direction of a party's ideology (e.g., either left or right) and the intensity with which a party advocates for its position. While both models are based on programmatic appeals, the latter has a considerably lower informational threshold. Hence, direction-intensity voting may be one adaptive strategy for voters to use in complex electoral spaces.

In addition to party ideology, I identify two additional heuristics that may help voters cope when electoral information is scarce. One major contender is the party leader heuristic or 'the personal vote' (Bean and Mughan 1989; Cain *et al.* 1987; Kaase 1994). Relying on sentiments towards party leaders is regarded as a low-information strategy as compared to voting based on policy. Not only does the party-leader heuristic require less information and information processing on the part of voters, but it has also been argued that it applies to 'new arrivals' on the party scene to a greater extent than it does to established parties (Ramonaite 2007; Grofman *et al.* 2000). Whereas the latter set of parties are rooted in the pre-existing social cleavages of an electorate, new parties make salient leaders' charisma. I test the implications of this argument for voting in unstable electoral spaces.

Finally, I explore the possibility that party instability itself can serve as a useful heuristic to voters. After all, change produces uncertainty about parties by interrupting their organisational continuity. Newcomers may be regarded with more wariness than newly formed mergers or splinter parties as the former are largely unknown to voters. Hence, we may reasonably conjecture that voters tend to *avoid* new and unstable parties in order to minimise risk and uncertainty. To the contrary of this thesis, however, case study research from Eastern Europe has shown that new parties have been particularly successful in elections (Sikk 2012). Given that these parties do not occupy new policy territory, their success has been attributed to their sheer novelty. In the pages that follow, I attempt to reconcile these conflicting expectations and test the extent to which voters use instability itself as an informational cue.

Heuristics for unstable parties: preliminary expectations

The ideology heuristic: Proximity and direction-intensity theories

In their seminal study, Lau and Redlawsk (2001, p. 953) explain the use of the political ideology heuristic as follows: 'If the salient characteristics of a particular politician are consistent with or representative of the prototypic [conservative party], say, then voters may readily infer that she is for a strong defense, low taxes, against government intervention in the economy, against abortion, and so on...' By relying on ideology alone, voters can infer party positions on a number of issues with relatively little knowledge about each party's exact stance on each policy. The ideology heuristic has one of the longest histories in political psychology and has gained widespread acceptance (Popkin 1991; Sniderman, Brody and Tetlock 1991; Lau and Redlawsk 2001, 2006; but see Bartels 1996).

Precisely *how* voters use ideology to elect parties has been less clear. In one model of ideology-based voting, voters choose based on their proximity to each party (Downs 1957). This model of voting posits that voters will select the party closest to them in policy space based on a rational calculation of policy distances to each party. Where both voters and parties can be represented by a point in a hypothetical policy space (usually, left-right), voters' decision-making is simply a matter of finding the party which is at the shortest policy distance from their own position.

An alternative model of ideology-based voting considers not only each voter's distance to each party but also the side of the ideological spectrum on which the voter finds herself (Rabinowitz and Macdonald 1989). The directional theory of issue voting predicts that voters will select parties whose positions are on the same side of the policy space and will prefer parties with more 'intense' positions on that side.[2] In contrast to the proximity model, voters are thought to select parties not on the grounds of objective policy issues or straightforward calculations of policy distances between each party and their own position but rather on their emotional responses to party appeals. While in both the proximity and the direction-intensity models voters decide based on ideology, the way in which ideology is used by the voter differs significantly. The proximity model posits a straightforward, *rational* calculation of policy distances while the direction-intensity model instead postulates an *emotional* response to the direction and intensity of party messages.

To appreciate how different these two perspectives on vote choice are, it is useful to compare the predictions they generate in the following scenario: imagine a policy space, as depicted in Figure 5.1, ranging from –5 to 5, where three parties (party A at –1, party B and 4 and party C at 5) compete for the ballots of two voters (voter Z at 1 and voter W at 3). The proximity model predicts that voters Z and W would select parties A and B, respectively, such that the absolute distance between voters and parties is minimised. Notice that in this scenario, voter Z selects party A, even though the party's position is opposite in direction from voter Z's position. In contrast, the directional theory of voting predicts that both voters would select party C, as the *directional* distance between voters and parties is maximised.[3] Party C is not only on the same side of the policy space, but its position is also the most 'intense' in that direction.

How may these theories apply when voters face unstable parties? The key to answering this question is the assertion that the proximity model requires *more* information on the part of voters than does the direction-intensity model

---

2. Formally, the model estimates the impact of an issue on an individual based on (1) the directional compatibility of the individual and the party and (2) the intensity levels of the individual and the candidate: Direction_intensity = Partylocation – Neutralpoint * Voterlocation – Neutralpoint.

3. Using Rabinowitz and Macdonald's formula above, the directional distances between voter Z and party A is $(-1 - 0)*(1 - 0)$, or –1; between voter Z and party B is 4; Z and C is 5. Similarly, between voter W and parties A, B and C, the directional distances are –3, 12 and 15, respectively.

Figure 5.1: Modes of ideological voting: proximity and direction-intensity compared

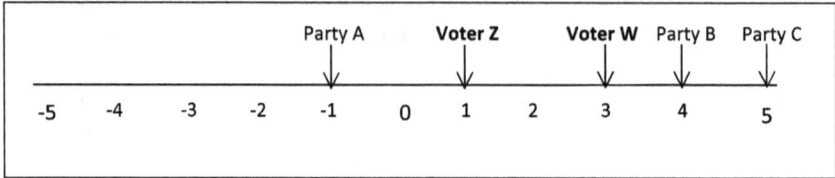

Note: This policy space ranges from −5 to 5 with a middle point at 0. There are three parties: Party A at −1, Party B and 4 and Party C at 5 that compete for the votes of Voter Z at 1 and Voter W at 3. The proximity model would predict that Voter Z casts a ballot for party A and Voter W for Party B. The direction-intensity model would predict that both voters cast a ballot for Party C.

(Rabinowitz and MacDonald 1989).[4] According to the proximity model, voters will compare their own positions to those of parties, and to do this, voters will need knowledge of parties' locations in policy space (*see* Chapter Four). In contrast, in the directional model voters need only diffuse perceptions of parties' positions; their task is to evaluate in which *direction* parties want to move the status quo and the *intensity* with which they advocate for such a change. The direction-intensity model of voting is cognitively and informationally less demanding than the proximity model because the former does not entail knowledge of parties' exact positions (Macdonald *et al.* 1995). The assertion that the direction-intensity model requires less information has received empirical support. Previous research shows systematic differences in the use of proximity and directional rules when voting for incumbent and challenger parties, respectively (Cho and Endersby 2003; Merril and Grofman 1997; 1999).[5] Because citizens are familiar with incumbents' positions to a greater extent than with challengers' positions, the proximity model is better suited to explaining vote choice for incumbents while the directional model explains better voters' decision to elect challengers.

It is therefore plausible that the relative performance of the proximity and direction-intensity models of voting will vary across parties as a function of the complexity and clarity of parties' electoral appeals. Where party messages are less clear due to a greater amount of new information which is not as easily attributable to a source – as I've argued is the case for unstable parties – we can expect voters to face higher information barriers (*see* Chapter Two). In voting for unstable parties, voters may be less likely to rely on their ideological proximity to parties as those positions are less clear to begin with (Expectation 1A). New and transformed parties are less familiar or are completely unknown to voters. As a result, voters have only a diffuse sense of their location in policy space. In contrast, when party messages are familiar and constant – as in the case of long-running, established

---

4. Note that voters' levels of political sophistication does not influence which rule they use (Macdonald *et al.* 1995).

5. However, others have failed to find an effect in Belgian elections (Maddens and Hajnal 2001).

parties – we can expect voters to continue using proximity considerations in casting a ballot. The results in Chapter Four, that voters are generally less familiar with the positions of new and transformed parties, are congruent with these expectations.

The flip-side of my argument is that voters will rely on direction-intensity appeals to a greater degree when casting a ballot for new or newly transformed parties (Expectation 1B). The research reviewed above suggests that direction-intensity voting is a low-information strategy of electoral decision-making as compared to ideological proximity. When faced with parties that send unclear messages, voters may adapt to this cognitively taxing information environment with a greater reliance on direction-intensity appeals. While voters are generally less capable of pinpointing unstable parties' ideological positions, they may nonetheless be able to discern unstable parties direction in policy space (left or right) and the extremity, or intensity, of the party's position. Together the differences in information required by the proximity and direction-intensity models, respectively, imply that the latter theory will better explain vote choice for unstable parties than the former.

The party leader heuristic

Moving away from programmatic appeals, we can further consider valence appeals based on voters' liking of political leaders. According to some accounts, democratic elections are becoming increasingly personalised (Andersen and Evans 2003; Evans and Andersen 2005; Poguntke and Webb 2005; but see Karvonen 2010). Candidate-centred, or personalised, campaigns imply a shift away from the programmatic appeals of political parties and towards the personalities of individual candidates (Poguntke and Webb 2005; Rahat and Sheafer 2007). The personalisation of electoral campaigns has manifested itself in the growing impact of leader effects on voting, or what has been labelled as casting a 'personal vote' (Bean and Mughan 1989; Cain *et al.* 1987; Kaase 1994). However, comparative analyses of leader effects in voting have produced some mixed results with regard to their spread (Karvonen 2010). Namely, many studies have failed to produce evidence that leader evaluations strongly determine the vote choice (Anderson and Brettschneider 2003; Curtice and Hunjan 2006; Graetz and McAllister 1987; Karvonen 2010). Still a number of articles show evidence of increasing candidate effects in voting (Andersen and Evans 2003; Arian and Shamir 2001; Evans and Andersen 2005; Garzia 2013; Graetz and McAllister 1987; Rahat and Sheafer 2007).

To parse out differences in candidate effects across elections, researchers have examined variation in the features of electoral and party systems at the national level. In investigating the impact of institutional rules and the political environment, Curtice and Hunjan (2006) find that leader assessments in majoritarian parliamentary systems are more important than in PR systems. McAllister (1996) brings forth evidence for a greater impact of leader effects on voting in polarised elections where larger parties are more prominent. When it comes to valence appeals, Klingemann and Wessels (2009) distinguish between party-liking and leader-liking. They find that in presidential election systems, the focus is primarily on candidate-liking while in electoral systems based on party voting, the primary focus is on party-liking. In congruence with Klingemann and Wessels, Tverdova (2011) concludes that voters use their feelings of representation by party in PR systems while in majoritarian systems they rely on their feelings of representation by political leaders. Contrary to previous research, she finds no evidence of country-level variables (e.g., party system polarisation, age of democracy, presidential or parliamentary structure of government) exerting an effect on partisan or candidate-centred voting.

In addition to country-level variables, Tverdova was one of the first to examine how the strength of candidate effects varies by *party* characteristics. She cites evidence that feeling well represented by a candidate matters more when voting for a younger party than for an established one. What is more, other party characteristics were not found to relate to the strength of candidate-based voting (e.g., party ideology, party size). Consistent with Tverdova, Ramonaite (2007, p. 91) finds that while established parties enjoy partisan loyalties motivated by 'value orientations, emotional engagement and group solidarity,' new parties generally lack deep social roots. To compensate, new parties will make salient the personalities of their leaders. A case study of Estonia corroborates these claims (Grofman *et al.* 2000). New Estonian parties formed around leaders instead of durable issues, lacking both organisational permanency and voter attachments. As the rate of formation of new parties in Estonia declined and major parties stabilised, programmatic competition along left-right ideology began to solidify. Though the study was based on a single case, the findings would suggest a rate of association between the rate of formation of new parties and the degree to which electoral campaigns centre on political personalities.

Some anecdotal evidence, too, offers support for the thesis that new parties may rely on feelings toward parties and candidates and further reveals a possible causal mechanism for this relationship. New parties from the early elections in Poland were a case in point as both party organisations and their leaders engaged in anti-party and anti-politics rhetoric emphasising political personalities instead. Some parties presented themselves as 'non-parties': the Civic Platform ran as a 'platform' rather than a party, and 'civic' rather than political. Like many other new parties, Samoobrana ran on anti-establishment rhetoric which was difficult to maintain once the party was elected into government. Moreover, new party leaders preferred to present themselves as 'professionals' rather than politicians. A prime example of this trend was former Polish President Lech Wałęsa. When new parties appeal on political personalities, it is arguably easier for voters to collect information on leaders' socio-cultural backgrounds than their policy commitments. The former is made more readily available in highly personalised electoral campaigns. While only anecdotal, this evidence nonetheless points to a potential causal mechanism between the entry of new parties and the propensity of voters to cast a personal vote. If new parties rely to a greater degree on the charisma of their leaders than on substantive policy issues, as case study research suggests, then the information new parties make available about themselves is more conducive to casting a personal vote.

Anecdotal evidence from Polish elections as well as comparative evidence on the effects of party age both suggest that the strength of candidate effects in voting will vary across political parties as a function of how embedded each party is in social and political cleavages. Because anti-establishment rhetoric seems to fade away with time, we can conjecture that new political formations will be particularly susceptible to candidate effects (Expectation 2A). We can argue further that valence appeals require a lower level of information on the part of voters because voters can rely on their gut feelings towards leaders rather than on detailed policy information (Brady and Sniderman 1985; Clarke 2009; Marcus *et al.* 2000). Voters can simply ask themselves, 'Do I like this party leader or not?' Because the party leader heuristic is a low-information strategy of voting, we can expect more generally that voters will rely on valence appeals as a coping strategy in complex electoral environments. Therefore, it is plausible that candidate appeals are stronger when voting for transformed than stable parties in general (Expectation 2B).

While anecdotal evidence of candidate effects among new parties is abundant, thus far we lack a formal test of the strength of these effects for new and transformed parties. Testing the expectations outlined above will provide such a test. Furthermore, testing these expectations can help distil the mixed evidence produced by the literature on the personalisation of politics (cf. Karvonen 2010). If party instability serves as a moderating factor in the strength of leader effects, then taking account of party changes can help explain puzzling variations in the personal vote both across elections and across parties within the same election.

Party instability as a heuristic

The final coping mechanism I consider here is the use of party instability as an informational cue, or what I label the 'party instability heuristic.' Voters decide between parties based on their characteristics (e.g., their ideology, how likeable their leaders are), and we have reasons to suspect that the history of the party carries valuable information in and of itself. Namely, existing parties imply stability and continuity while newcomers and newly transformed parties imply a break with the past. How voters use such information is not obvious. While we may imagine that voters will attempt to minimise risk by supporting established parties, at least some previous research has argued that voters are in fact *attracted* to the novelty of new party formations. I develop expectations based on each of these insights in turn.

On one hand, it is plausible that voters are reluctant to choose new or newly transformed parties due to the uncertainty associated with lesser known or completely unknown electoral alternatives. This expectation is motivated by studies suggesting that voters are risk averse and generally seek to minimise uncertainty (Alvarez 1998; Koch 2003). The evidence brought to bear on this claim is based on voters' uncertainty with regard to parties' *policy* positions. Voters are reluctant to choose parties whose positions they consider uncertain because those positions may in fact be far from the voter's own set of preferences (Koch 2003). One consequence of this is that parties with more extremist positions, that are nonetheless clearer to the voter, are more likely to be elected into office. Ezrow *et al.* (2014) have recently demonstrated this to be the case in the post-socialist democracies of Europe. One factor that systematically shapes voters' levels of certainty about parties' positions is their incumbency. The incumbency advantage is in part due to voters' familiarity with incumbents' positions and their uncertainty about challengers' positions (cf. Bernhardt and Ingberman 1985; Ingberman 1989).

While extant research has convincingly demonstrated that uncertainty about parties' policy positions weakens their electoral support, we have little knowledge of how uncertainty stemming from parties' organisational changes shapes the vote. Due to party instability, voters face increased uncertainty in several respects. First, voters need to gather additional information on newcomers. Since such information may not be readily forthcoming, we saw in Chapter Four that voters are generally less knowledgeable about parties that have undergone instability. Given the scarcity of information about newcomers, voters may be reluctant to entrust new and unstable parties with policymaking power. Second, the lack of an established record of governance or in opposition may be to newcomers' disadvantage because it creates uncertainty about their commitment to their proposed policy programs. As Clarke (2009, p. 48) writes, 'In general, past performance will be preferred to future promises, because information about performance is more reliable.' Lacking a record of governance, new parties introduce information uncertainty with respect to government formation as well as new parties' potential role in opposition (Grotz and Weber 2015). If elected into office, their politics are more difficult to predict than those of long-running, established parties. As a result of uncertainty due to both lower knowledge of parties' policy positions and new and transformed parties' limited record of governance, voters may generally shy away from unknown or lesser known electoral alternatives and choose stable, established parties instead (Expectation 3A).

Contrary to this expectation, at least one scholar has argued that voters may in fact be attracted to new parties – not for their novel policy positions but simply for being new. In a case study of four Baltic parties, Sikk (2012) finds that the emergence of both new party formations and transformed parties was not related to an incentive to represent new social cleavages, issues or spaces on the ideological continuum (cf. Harmel and Robertson 1985; Müller-Rommel 2002). Instead, Sikk argues that voters were attracted to the parties due to their sheer novelty: 'newness has been an appealing project for new and rejuvenating parties everywhere' (465).[6] The new and transformed parties in Sikk's analysis did not propose radical alternatives to the status quo but rather occupied the ideological

---

6. By 'newness', Sikk (2012) means both new parties appearing on the ballot for the first time and existing parties that have 'rejuvenated' by changing their organisational structure (for example, merged with another party).

spaces of mainstream parties. As a consequence, Sikk contends that new party formations carried a 'low risk of scaring off potential supporters' (478).

Sikk's findings thus add an important nuance to Expectation 3A which states that, no matter what, party instability may turn voters away. The case study conducted by Sikk qualifies and, to an extent, challenges this expectation in two important ways. First, Sikk takes into account new parties' policy positions. As long as new parties do not take extreme positions, they would arguably not present a risky alternative to preexisting parties. When new parties' policy positions overlap with mainstream parties' positions, then they carry considerably less risk and uncertainty. Second, Sikk casts party instability in a positive light. Rather than presenting voters with a risk or a higher level of uncertainty, 'rejuvenated' parties in and of themselves may be attractive to voters. We could argue further that the novelty of these parties may stimulate interest in voters who would then familiarise themselves with the new and transformed parties and in doing so reduce their uncertainty. Research in political psychology has demonstrated that novelty in the political campaign stimulates voters' attention and encourages political learning (Marcus and MacKuen 1993). Following these claims, we can formulate an alternative expectation: as long as unstable parties do not take extreme ideological stances, they will be more attractive to voters than pre-existing parties (Expectation 3B).

Testing these mixed expectations presents an interesting and important test. While examples of electorally successful, new parties with mainstream policy positions are abundant in European elections, we have little knowledge of how voters use information on party novelty in their electoral calculus.[7] In a small-N case study, Sikk found that party novelty has a role in the electoral success of parties that is separate from parties' programmatic positions. Sikk's findings have empirical implications at the micro level of analysis, for voters' electoral decision-making, which have thus far not be empirically tested. Furthermore, there has been no evaluation of the extent to which Sikk's conclusion holds outside the Baltic countries. In a large-N comparative analysis, I test how information about party instability is used by voters.

Data and method of analysis

To test the hypotheses of this chapter, I combine survey evidence of voting with data on instability, both in its type and degree, for each party. By combining evidence at the voter-party level of analysis, I am able to test the expectations outlined above. Namely, do voters shy away from unstable parties, or are they attracted to them for their sheer novelty (Expectations 3A-B)? Do voters rely on proximity considerations to a lesser degree when electing new and transformed parties (1A)? Do they rely on direction-intensity appeals instead (1B)? And what

---

7. For example, see the Slovak Smer (Haughton 2004; Rybář and Deegan-Krause 2008), Citizens for European Development of Bulgaria (Stefanova 2008; Stoychev 2008), the Polish Civic Platform and Law and Justice (Szczerbiak 2002; Szczerbiak 2004), Forza Italia (Farrell 1995; Hopkin and Paolucci 1999) and the French New Centre (Sikk 2012).

is the role of valence appeals when voters choose between stable and unstable parties (2A-B)? In testing these expectations, I examine both the *type* of instability parties undergo (e.g., new formations, merged parties, splinters and so on) and the *overall* degree of change in each party.

To measure voting behaviour, I use survey data from the Comparative Study of Electoral Systems (CSES). To test the first set of expectations, I estimate the absolute distance in left-right ideology between (1) the voter's self-placement on the left-right ideological continuum and (2) political experts' placement of each party on the same scale.[8] Directional distance is estimated with the formula of Rabinowitz and MacDonald (1989) by relying on the experts' placement of each party and voter self-placements. To test the second set of expectations, I use a measure of party leader sympathy. Respondents rated the degree to which they liked or disliked each party leader on a scale from 0 to 10, where higher values indicate more positive feelings.[9] The models also include individual-level control variables for age, gender and level of education.

To test the final set of expectations, I include a number of party-level variables described in detail in Chapter Three. I first test the expectations separately for each category of party change. I then include a measure of the *total* number of organisational changes in *each* party. In addition, I control for party age (own estimation). To control for the extreme ideological position, I include a set of binary variables for party family (ecology, communist, socialist, social democratic, left liberal, liberal, right liberal, Christian democratic, conservative, national, agrarian, ethnic, regional, independent and other party families (source: CSES)). Since voters are likely more familiar with parties that were in government, I include a binary indicator of incumbent status.

Method of analysis

The resulting data matrix is stacked at the individual per party level and contains repeated observations on individual. The statistical technique I apply is a conditional logit model grouped by individual (McFadden, 1974). This tool presents several advantages over alternative individual-level models and allows me to test the expectations elaborated above. Most importantly, the utility function of the model enables voters to compare the attributes of multiple parties, including their own policy distance from each party and the degree to which they like each party's leader. Alternative individual-level models would not allow me to model the vote choice as a function of utility for *each* party. The conditional logit model allows me to model party attributes, such as age, instability and like-dislike sentiments of

8. Recall that in Estonia-2011, CSES expert placements of parties were hugely off from both the average placement by voters and an independent expert survey (Vowles, Hellwig and Coffey 2009). Hence, I have used the Vowles *et al.* placements rounded to the nearest digit. See the Appendix for more information.

9. 'And what do you think of the presidential candidates/party? After I read the name of a presidential candidate, please rate them on a scale from 0 to 10, where 0 means you strongly dislike that candidate and 10 means that you strongly like that candidate.'

party leaders, which would otherwise not be possible. Employing the conditional logit model is therefore critical to testing the hypotheses of this chapter.

To express the model formally, we can denote election study with an s and the dependent variable, vote choice, with values, 0, 1, 2, ..., J_s where, 1 though J_s denote the modelled parties and 0 denotes voting for one of the unmodelled parties.[10] The utility individual n receives from voting for option j is given by, $u_{nj} = \beta'x_{nj} + \varepsilon_{nj}$ (6.2), where ε_{nj} are distributed *iid* extreme value. The independent variables here, x_{nj}, vary over both individuals and choices (e.g., party characteristics), but only variables that vary over choices can enter into the utility function. That is, demographic characteristics, such as age, and country-level characteristics, such as electoral system type, do not affect the choice of the individual n; these types of variables equally shift the utilities of all choices for each individual.

Extending the utility function to the conditional logit model, we have

$$Pr(y_n = j \mid x_{n1},...,x_{nJs}) = \frac{e^{\beta'x_{nj}}}{\sum_{k=0}^{J_s} e^{\beta'x_{nk}}}$$ (6.3), for $j \in (0, 1, ..., Js)$. A number of different

covariates constitute x_{nj}: ideological distance between the individual and each party, the individual's like-dislike feeling towards each party's leader, and each party's history of organisational change. In addition, the model allows me to control for party family and party age. To assess the effect of party instability in each party on the relationships between ideology and party and leader feelings, on one hand, and party instability, on the other hand, I use interaction terms. To account for the fact that demographic groups may differ in their relative preference for incumbent parties and their relative preferences for the attributes captured by the party family dummies, I include interaction between demographic characteristics with the variable party age.

Empirical findings

Overall, the empirical analyses offer substantial support for the hypotheses developed in this chapter. The analyses below demonstrate that direction-intensity appeals can better predict a vote for a new or a newly transformed party while programmatic appeals do better for stable parties. Furthermore, leader appeals were stronger when casting a ballot for unstable parties than long-standing parties. Finally, in line with Expectation 3A, voters use party instability as a cue, such that they shy away from unstable parties. These results are discussed in detail below.

Upon initial examination, the empirical results hold up to face validity. As we would expect, voters were significantly more likely to re-elect incumbents parties (odds are 28 per cent higher; $p<0.05$) as well as parties closer to them in policy space (one additional point on the left-right continuum reduced the odds of voting

---

10. Note that the choice set of parties varies across elections. This is consistent with McFadden's description of the conditional logit model, and standard statistical software accommodates this feature (See Kayser and Peress 2012).

Table 5.1: Vote choice: party instability as a heuristic

	(1)	(2)	(3)	(4)
Left-right distance	−0.470***	−0.469***	−0.465***	−0.463***
	0.0259	0.0257	0.0262	0.0260
Incumbent	0.249*	0.231+	0.196+	0.176
	0.1266	0.1255	0.1172	0.1180
New party	−0.108		0.298	
	0.3137		0.3307	
Merged	**−0.416+**		**−0.552***	
	0.2521		**0.2313**	
JL Entry	−0.045		−0.074	
	0.2884		0.2373	
Splinter	−0.273		0.216	
	0.2625		0.2830	
JL Exit	**−1.110***		**−1.302***	
	0.2809		**0.3806**	
Party instability		**−0.323****		**−0.288***
(total)		**0.1167**		**0.1181**
Party age	0.003+	0.003+	−0.001	−0.001
	0.0017	0.0016	0.0016	0.0016
Party family *(Reference-ecology)*				
Communist			−0.337	−0.320
			0.4136	0.3947
Socialist			0.903***	0.873***
			0.1895	0.1819
Social-democratic			1.200***	1.174***
			0.2011	0.1920
Left-liberal			−0.459+	−0.443+
			0.2397	0.2374
Liberal			0.584**	0.551**
			0.1846	0.1802
Right-liberal			0.514*	0.529*
			0.2388	0.2309
Christian democratic			0.757***	0.698***
			0.1556	0.1511
Conservative			0.915***	0.908***
			0.2374	0.2319

Table 5.1 (*continued*)

	(1)	(2)	(3)	(4)
National			0.739*	0.731*
			0.3390	0.3255
Agrarian			0.176	0.163
			0.2589	0.2622
Ethnic			0.019	0.030
			0.1884	0.1895
Regional			−0.987*	−1.012*
			0.4957	0.4894
Religious			−2.537***	−2.042***
			0.3527	0.2248
Independent			−0.501	−0.428
			0.3557	0.4460
Other			−0.090	0.370
			0.3408	0.3446
Log-likelihood	−79449	−79665	−75559	−75973
AIC	158920	159345	151169	151991
N	317444	317444	317444	317444

Note: Coefficients and standard errors from a conditional (fixed-effects) logistic regression model of vote choice are reported. The sample contains 317,444 respondent-party pairs from 55 elections. All models include interactions between party age and socio-demographic characteristics (age, gender and education) [not displayed]. Coefficient estimates are maximum likelihood unstandardised coefficients. Analyses were performed in Stata 12 with the .clogit command. $+p<0.1$, $*p < 0.05$, $**p < 0.01$, $***p < 0.001$

a party by 37.5 per cent; $p<0.001$). Older parties were at a slight advantage; each additional year increased the party's odds by 0.003 per cent ($p<0.1$).

I first examine the predictive power of party instability on the vote choice. Namely, do voters use party instability as an informational cue? The third set of expectations suggests that voters may be more reluctant to elect new and unstable parties, or that alternatively voters may be attracted to those newcomers who are not ideologically extreme (Expectations 3A-B). Model 1 in Table 5.1 shows two categories of instability to have an overall negative effect on voting outcomes: mergers and joint lists. Parties that merged with another party before the election had odds that were 34 per cent lower to be voted for ($p<0.1$), controlling for other covariates. Parties that left a joint list had odds that were 67 per cent lower than stable parties ($p<0.1$). Coefficients of all categories of instability have a negative sign but do not reach statistical significance. In Model 2, the overall number of party changes also has a statistically significant effect; one additional party change decreases the odds of being elected by 28 per cent as compared to stable

Table 5.2: Mean differences in per cent votes received by party instability

Underwent change	New party	Splinter party	Merged party	Joint list entry	Joint list exit	Any change
Yes	7.6	7.7	21.5	13.3	11.2	14.3
	(n=97)	(n=86)	(n=209)	(n=281)	(n=165)	(n=584)
No	29.5	29.4	28.9	31.1	29.9	36.0
	(n=1453)	(n=1544)	(n=1358)	(n=1286)	(n=1402)	(n=983)
Absolute	21.9	21.7	7.4	17.7	18.7	21.7**
Difference	(n=1550)	(n=1544)	(n=1567)	(n=1567)	(n=1567)	(n=1567)

Note: **$p<0.05$

parties ($p<0.01$). Following Sikk (2012), I next test these results against the extremity of political parties. These results hold up well after controlling for party family (Models 3–4, Table 5.1). Overall, the analyses suggest that voters *do* use information about party instability, and they do so to avoid unstable parties rather than elect them into office.[11]

It is important to emphasise that the CSES includes information only about major parties.[12] Parties that were electorally marginal do not figure into the CSES data base. As a result, the analyses above allow us to test whether or not instability influences the electoral results of major parties; yet we cannot say much about how party instability affects the electoral fortunes of marginal parties that did not pass the electoral threshold. To remedy this, I use the party-level data described in Chapter Three to measure electoral success against the history of party change for all parties that pass the 1 per cent threshold. Table 5.2 presents a formal test of the equality of mean votes received by category of party instability. Although for the separate categories of party change the t-test does not reject the null hypothesis that the means are equal, we see substantial differences in magnitude. Overall, the vote share of new and transformed parties is considerably lower than that of established parties. The mean differences range from 7 per cent less for merged parties to 21 per cent less for new or splinter parties. When we compare parties that have undergone any type of change to stable parties, we see that the vote share of the former are 21 per cent lower than that of the latter ($p<0.05$). These results are congruent with the findings presented in Table 5.1. On average, voters seem reluctant to elect parties that are either new or have transformed since the previous election, lending support to Expectation 3A.

The next set of models tests the extent to which voters select parties on the basis of their programmatic proximity to their own positions. As we would expect,

---

11. I modeled these relationships separately for Central and Eastern Europe and Western Europe, respectively. In both regions overall party instability was associated negatively with the vote ($p<0.05$). The types of party transformations that voters avoided differed in the two regions. In CEE, mergers and joint list exists were negatively associated with vote choice ($p<0.05$). In WE, voters were more reluctant to elect new parties, mergers and splinters ($p<0.2$).

12. Normally, electoral information on the 5 to 7 major parties will be included in the CSES files (in a few cases, up to 9 parties are included).

Table 5.3: Vote choice: ideological proximity

	(1)	(2)	(3)	(4)	(5)
Left-right distance	−0.469***	−0.473***	−0.467***	−0.473***	−0.471***
	0.0259	0.0264	0.0261	0.0260	0.0257
Incumbent	0.249*	0.249*	0.250*	0.250*	0.249*
	0.1265	0.1266	0.1266	0.1266	0.1265
New party	0.092	−0.114	−0.109	−0.111	−0.108
	0.4400	0.3131	0.3135	0.3139	0.3126
Merged	−0.415	−0.556*	−0.419	−0.417+	−0.415+
	0.2535	0.2536	0.2553	0.2518	0.2524
JL Entry	−0.045	−0.044	0.137	−0.045	−0.045
	0.2882	0.2882	0.3376	0.2879	0.2883
Splinter	−0.274	−0.275	−0.274	−0.624*	−0.273
	0.2623	0.2608	0.2623	0.2641	0.2624
JL Exit	−1.125***	−1.109***	−1.123***	−1.108***	−1.141**
	0.2707	0.2801	0.2745	0.2801	0.3605
Party age	0.003+	0.003+	0.003+	0.003+	0.003+
	0.0017	0.0017	0.0017	0.0017	0.0017
Left-right distance* New party	−0.134				
	0.0944				
Left-right distance* Merged		**0.085***			
		0.0374			
Left-right distance* JL Entry			−0.104		
			0.0848		
Left-right distance* Splinter				**0.180****	
				0.0560	
Left-right distance* JL Exit					0.020
					0.0824
Log-likelihood	−79436	−79438	−79435	−79429	−79449
AIC	158895	158900	158893	158883	158922
N	317444	317444	317444	317444	317444

Note: Coefficients and standard errors from a conditional (fixed-effects) logistic regression model of vote choice are reported. The sample contains 317,444 respondent-party pairs from 55 elections. All models include interactions between party age and socio-demographic characteristics (age, gender and education) [not displayed]. Coefficient estimates are maximum likelihood unstandardised coefficients. Analyses were performed in Stata 12 with the .clogit command. +$p<0.1$, *$p < 0.05$, **$p < 0.01$, ***$p < 0.001$

we see a negative relationship between increasing left-right distance and the vote; with every additional point that separates a party from a voter, the voters' odds of selecting a stable party decrease by 0.62 ($p<0.001$; Model 1 in Table 5.1). If voters rely on proximity considerations to a lower extent when voting for unstable parties, then the interaction coefficient between ideological distance and instability will be positive; the more instability, the less reliant voters will be on proximity considerations. In Table 5.3, we see that this is the case for two types of party instability: both party mergers and party splinters condition the effect of left-right proximity on the vote. When parties either merge or splint, voters are significantly less likely to rely on proximity considerations to inform their electoral choice. When a party has undergone a merger, a voter's odds of selecting the party on left-right proximity considerations are 8 per cent higher compared to stable parties ($p<0.001$). When a party is a splinter of a previous party, the odds of selecting the party on proximity grounds are 21 per cent higher compared to stable parties ($p<0.001$). The interactions of proximity distance and the remainder of party instability categories do not reach statistical significance at $p<0.1$. Overall, we find empirical support for a weaker effect of programmatic distance considerations on the vote when parties emerge from splinters or when they merge with other parties (Expectation 1A).

Next, I test whether direction-intensity appeals can help us understand the vote for unstable parties. If direction-intensity is a low-information voting strategy, as argued by Rabinowitz and MacDonald (1989), then it is plausible that voters rely on direction-intensity appeals to a greater degree when parties transform and do not send clear party cues (Expectation 1B). As expected, voters maximise direction-intensity appeals; voters' odds of selecting a stable party increase by 1.14 with each additional direction-intensity unit.[13] Table 5.4 presents models which provide a formal test of the interaction between direction-intensity distance and party instability; if the interaction term is positive, then party instability will reinforce the relationship between direction-intensity appeals and the vote. This is the case for two types of party change: new parties and joint lists (Models 1 and 5). When a party is new, voters' odds of relying on direction-intensity appeals are 6 per cent higher as compared to preexisting parties ($p<0.001$). When a party has recently left a joint list, the odds of electing the party on direction-intensity grounds are 14 per cent higher as compared to stable parties. The interaction of direction-intensity and the remainder of party instability categories did not reach statistical significance at $p<0.1$. In the case of joint lists and new parties, we find evidence that corroborates Expectation 1B – voters rely on direction-intensity appeals to a higher degree when parties transform.

Finally, we turn to testing the strength of leader effects on the vote. If candidate liking is a low-information strategy of voting, then we can expect that voters are more likely to rely on valence appeals when party cues are not effectively communicated, as I have argued is the case for new and transformed parties (Chapter Two). In line

---

13. This estimate is based on a model without interaction effects where the logged-odds coefficient on leader-liking is 0.48 ($p<0.001$).

Table 5.4: Vote choice: direction-intensity voting

	(1)	(2)	(3)	(4)	(5)
Direction-intensity	0.132***	0.131***	0.131***	0.133***	0.131***
	0.0123	0.0123	0.0119	0.0124	0.0122
Incumbent	0.391**	0.390**	0.392**	0.393**	0.389**
	0.1305	0.1303	0.1301	0.1303	0.1302
New party	0.181	0.240	0.232	0.235	0.233
	0.3149	0.2972	0.2930	0.2982	0.2888
Merged	−0.166	−0.218	−0.181	−0.170	−0.194
	0.3020	0.3504	0.3107	0.3053	0.3305
JL Entry	−0.117	−0.121	−0.249	−0.119	−0.121
	0.3188	0.3180	0.2834	0.3186	0.3184
Splinter	−0.426*	−0.478*	−0.443*	−0.360	−0.474*
	0.2010	0.1925	0.1948	0.2609	0.1880
JL Exit	−0.997***	−1.026***	−1.046***	−1.008***	−1.314***
	0.2541	0.2516	0.2428	0.2544	0.2789
Direction-intensity *	**0.065+**				
New party	**0.0372**				
Direction-intensity *		0.037			
Merged		0.0515			
Direction-intensity *			0.039		
JL Entry			0.0539		
Direction-intensity *				−0.019	
Splinter				0.0205	
Direction-intensity *					**0.136***
JL Exit					**0.0681**
Party Instability (total) Direction-intensity *					
Party age	0.004*	0.004*	0.004*	0.004*	0.004*
	0.0019	0.0019	0.0019	0.0019	0.0019

Table 5.4 (*continued*)

	(1)	(2)	(3)	(4)	(5)
Log-likelihood	–82283	–82283	–82269	–82293	–82234
AIC	164590	164591	164561	164610	164493
N	317444	317444	317444	317444	317444

Note: Coefficients and standard errors from a conditional (fixed-effects) logistic regression model of vote choice are reported. The sample contains 317,444 respondent-party pairs from 55 elections. All models include interactions between party age and socio-demographic characteristics (age, gender and education) [not displayed]. Coefficient estimates are maximum likelihood unstandardised coefficients. Analyses were performed in Stata 12 with the .clogit command. +p<0.1, *p < 0.05, **p < 0.01, ***p < 0.001

Table 5.5: Vote choice: leader valence appeals

	(1)	(2)	(3)	(4)
Left-right distance	–0.316***	–0.315***	–0.315***	–0.315***
	0.0473	0.0474	0.0474	0.0474
Incumbent	0.189	0.189	0.190	0.189
	0.2169	0.2170	0.2176	0.2170
Like party leader	0.480***	0.482***	0.483***	0.480***
	0.0779	0.0786	0.0791	0.0782
New party	–2.460***	–0.400	–0.401	–0.394
	0.4164	0.2974	0.2974	0.2998
Merged	–0.013	–0.142	–0.009	–0.008
	0.3058	0.5010	0.3050	0.3026
JL Entry	0.153	0.153	0.280	0.154
	0.4553	0.4561	0.5580	0.4563
Splinter	–0.113	–0.125	–0.127	–1.574+
	0.2347	0.2410	0.2408	0.8732
JL Exit	–3.008***	–3.005***	–3.005***	–3.007***
	0.1644	0.1639	0.1646	0.1645
Like * New party	**0.305***			
	0.0672			
Like * Merged		0.021		
		0.0481		
Like * JL Entry			–0.022	
			0.0624	
Like * Splinter				**0.204***
				0.1001

Table 5.5 (*continued*)

	(1)	(2)	(3)	(4)
Like * JL Exit				
Party age	0.003	0.003	0.003	0.003
	0.0026	0.0026	0.0026	0.0026
Log-likelihood	−31977	−32003	−32003	−31983
AIC	63977	64030	64030	63990
N	165427	165427	165427	165427

Note: Coefficients and standard errors from a conditional (fixed-effects) logistic regression model of vote choice are reported. The sample contains 165,427 respondent-party pairs from 33 elections. All models include interactions between party age and socio-demographic characteristics (age, gender and education) [not displayed]. A model for joint list exit was not included; after the sample size declined to 33 elections, no cases of joint list exit remained in the data set. Coefficient estimates are maximum likelihood unstandardised coefficients. Analyses were performed in Stata 12 with the .clogit command. +p<0.1, *$p < 0.05$, **$p < 0.01$, ***$p < 0.001$

with previous research, the odds of voting for a party increase by 62 per cent as a voter expresses more positive feelings towards a party's leader ($p<0.001$).[14] If instability in parties strengthens candidate effects in voting, the interaction term between candidate-liking and party instability will be positive. This is indeed the case for new parties and splinter parties (Models 1 and 3 in Table 5.5). When it comes to new parties, voters' odds of relying on feelings towards a party leader are 35 per cent higher than the odds of doing so when voting for stable parties ($p<0.001$). The odds of candidate effects are 23 per cent higher for splinter parties than stable parties ($p<0.001$). These results are congruent with past research which demonstrates that new parties rely to a greater extent on leader charisma in order to compensate for their lack of social roots (Grofman *et al.* 2000; Tverdova 2007; Ramonaite 2007). While these findings show substantially higher candidate effects for unstable parties, they should be taken with a grain of salt. In this final set of models, the sample size decreased drastically due to missing data on party leader sentiments.[15] In the resulting sample, only one to two parties undergo each type of party change, and there were no parties that emerged due to a joint list exit.

Conclusions

If voters tend to know less about party positions in erratic elections (Chapter Four), could alternative theories of electoral decision-making explain how voters decide

---

14. This estimate is based on a model without interaction effects where the coefficient on direction-intensity is 0.13 ($p<0.001$).

15. The survey item on party leader feelings was only asked in the first and third modules of the CSES. As a result, the sample declines from 55 to 33 elections.

as parties change? This chapter set out to chart the heuristics voters use in order to adapt to low-information environments characterised by party instability. I argued that voters may use several decision-making strategies when voting for new and transformed parties: direction-intensity appeals, feelings towards party leaders and information on party instability itself. The empirical analyses offered substantial support for many of the expectations laid out at the beginning of this chapter. First, when parties undergo changes between elections, voters use instability as a cue in and of itself, shying away from new and changed parties. Despite Sikk's (2005) conclusions about changed parties in the Baltic countries, micro-level and party-level evidence suggests that voters turn away from electoral alternatives that are unknown and therefore uncertain. Second, direction-intensity between voters and parties is a better predictor of vote choice as new parties emerge and existing parties transform. As voters tend to know less about transformed parties' policy stances (*see* Chapter Four), they rely on diffuse perceptions of party positions (namely, the direction and intensity of positions) which is less cognitively demanding. Finally, voters were more likely to be swayed by their gut feelings towards party leaders when voting for new and splinter parties than they were when voting for stable parties. These results are congruent with anecdotal evidence that new parties appeal to voters based on the political personalities of party leaders rather than policy positions.

These findings have important implications for citizen-elite linkages and representational outcomes. While lower levels of familiarity with parties' positions do not deter voters from electing new and unstable parties on programmatic appeals, to do so voters use political ideology in a distinctly different way. Namely, voters rely less on parties' exact positions in policy space and decide instead based on the direction and intensity of their appeals – information which is more accessible in low-information elections. On one hand, this constitutes good news; low-information environments do not necessarily prevent voters from using policy compatibility as a metric. On the other hand, as voters rely on the intensity of party appeals to cope in low-information elections, the elevated use of direction-intensity appeals also means that the emergence of new parties and the transformation of existing parties bring about the election of more ideologically extreme parties (cf. Hinich and Munger 1997). While many scholars have rung the alarm bell on extreme parties, there is evidence that new political formations become driven towards the mainstream once elected into parliament. Flanagan and Dalton (1984, p. 9) explain that new parties become 'socialised into the realities and limitations of effecting political change and the need for compromise to achieve any progress' (cf. Mudde 1996; Rydgren 2005). While taking more extreme positions increases new parties' chances of electoral success, electing extreme parties does not necessarily translate into radical politics, or at least not over the long haul.

The results of this chapter further imply that voters correctly identify risk and uncertainty in elections. Despite the four cases in the Baltics where new and transformed parties were elected into office, the general trend is that voters shy away from newcomers and transformed parties. When we examined a large sample of elections across Europe, on average new and unstable parties received 20 per cent per cent less in vote shares than long-running, stable parties. That voters are generally reluctant to elect newcomers spells good news for political representation. Not only are voters less familiar with unstable parties' policy programs, but they have little or no information on their performance in office.[16] Thus voting for new and unstable parties presents voters with a certain level of uncertainty. Given the higher electoral risk associated with unstable parties, voters' disinclination to hand over policymaking powers to newcomers constitutes a lucid and reasoned decision and is ultimately good news for political representation.

The empirical analyses from this chapter further show that, when it comes to new and splinter parties, the odds of relying on sentiments towards party leaders are 20 to 30 per cent higher than stable parties. These results are consistent with the argument that gut feelings towards political personalities constitute a feasible voting strategy in low-information elections. Taken to the macro level, the result of stronger candidate effects for new and transformed parties imply greater personalisation of politics in elections characterised by high levels of party instability. While the leader heuristic can be regarded as a rational voting strategy in low-information elections, the representational outcome it generates – an elevated personalisation of politics – is generally regarded as less desirable. Poguntke and Webb (2005, p. 22) explain that the personalisation of politics means that party leaders 'increasingly govern past their parties and [...] past the most important social forces which support them.' Parties founded on charismatic political personalities imply weak party organisations and little social bases behind them; once party leaders lose popularity, the party organisation is likely to dissolve, bringing about further instability. The personalisation of politics thus implies weaker parties that are more susceptible to instances of party change. By incentivising voters to rely on candidate heuristics, party instability triggers a vicious cycle of further instability.

In the following chapter I examine another coping strategy for low-information elections: the economic vote.

---

16. Some transformed parties (e.g., splinters) may have previously been part of a government. As I discuss in the following chapter, the organisational break in the party makes it harder for voters to judge whether or not the party's past record in governance is a good predictor of its future performance.

Chapter Six

Judging Competence: The Economic Vote

In the previous two chapters, I explored the implications of elections' complexity for voters' information seeking and use of heuristics. The analyses revealed that party instability depresses familiarity with electoral alternatives and encourages voters to use an alternative set of decision-making strategies suited to low-information environments. In this chapter I explore another potential coping mechanism – the economic vote.

Retrospective economic voting has long been held as a low-information strategy for casting a ballot (Key 1966; Fiorina 1981). The economic voter relies on a single and simple piece of information: the state of the economy. Conventional wisdom has it that voters need only assess the state of the economy in order to re-elect the incumbents or throw them out. Prospective voters, in contrast, need considerably more information (i.e., party positions) and cognitive effort (i.e., to estimate the compatibility of their own position with those offered by parties) to cast a ballot. As voters are hard pressed to identify the policy positions of transforming parties, one could reasonably expect that they rely on economic considerations instead. Motivated by the low-information logic of economic voting, I explore the extent to which voters employ retrospective economic evaluations as a voting strategy in elections characterised by party instability.

If we accept the low-information logic of the economic vote – which several studies have recently challenged[1] – a number of important questions remain unanswered. How do voters weigh the economic record of incumbents whose parties have split, abandoned joint lists or undergone other forms of instability? Is information on the state of the economy sufficient to cast an economic vote as parties transform? If the aim of the economic voter is to elect competent policymakers (Alesina and Rosenthal 1995), then the state of the economy will be just one important signal of competence. The economic voter will also need to take into account the uncertainty produced by party instability in judging the governing competences of competing parties. I argue that voters rely on retrospective evaluations of the economy only when they can safely assume that incumbents' past economic record is a good predictor of future performance.

Party instability puts a question mark on the link between parties' past economic record of governance and their potential performance in the future. Interrupting the continuity of party organisations, along with the leadership and membership changes this implies, instability introduces uncertainty about parties' competence

---

1. For example, see De Vries and Giger (2014), Fortunato and Stevenson (2013), and Hellwig and Marinova (2015). Below I discuss the evidence against the low-information logic of economic voting.

and subsequent performance. When parties split or leave an electoral alliance, for example, voters may have good reason to believe that their levels of competence will change. Voters may reasonably intuit that after a party transformation has taken place, prior information, like incumbents' past economic record, may no longer be a reliable indicator of the party's future performance. In contexts of high party instability, the retrospective evaluations of the economy are not necessarily a good indicator of future performance.

Considering how party instability shapes the economic vote should shed new light on the ongoing puzzle as to why electoral accountability is fulfilled only in some elections (cf. Lewis-Beck and Stegmaier 2013). The weak and inconsistent rates of economic voting have been attributed to voters' informational shortfalls, skewed perceptions of the governments' management of the economy or their displayed difficulty in gauging which political actors should be held accountable (e.g., Nadeau et al. 1999, 2000; Sanders and Gavin 2004; Powell and Whitten 1993; Whitten and Palmer 1999). Comparative research assumes that when voters do not cast an economic vote, it is because they are not able to do so. The unstated assumption is that economic voting is a universally optimal strategy of electing competent policy makers.

The argument developed in this chapter parts ways with the received wisdom in directly challenging the implicit assumption that economic voting is always desirable. The chapter illuminates one scenario – elections characterised by party instability – when voters may intentionally neglect, or give less weight to, information on economic performance. Evidence that voters do so would signal reasoned decision-making rather than informational shortfalls. Indeed as parties transform, an economic vote would not necessarily bring about the election of competent policymakers into office or incentivise good management of the national economy. The findings from this chapter should push scholars to reconsider the widely-held assumption that economic performance should always serve as the basis of the vote.

To situate this chapter in the extant literature on economic retrospective voting, I begin by reviewing the current state of knowledge and particularly the low-information logic of the economic vote. I then elaborate on the mechanisms by which party instability potentially conditions electoral decision-making based on retrospective evaluations of government performance. I conduct two sets of analyses to test the empirical implications of my argument: at the micro level, I analyse survey data from the Comparative Study of Electoral Systems (CSES); and at the election level, I analyse macroeconomic indicators and electoral results. Controlling for variation in the clarity of responsibility of institutions, I find evidence that party instability is associated with lower rates of retrospective voting and electoral accountability. Voters are less likely to rely on their retrospective evaluations of government performance when parties change. As a consequence, incumbents are less likely to be sanctioned for their economic record. I conclude by discussing the implications of these results for low-information decision-making and political representation more broadly.

The low-information rationality of economic voting

Economic retrospective voting has long been considered a low-information strategy of casting a ballot (Key 1966; Fiorina 1981). If policy outputs are desirable, citizens re-elect the incumbent government; otherwise, they cast a ballot for the opposition. Voters are thought to need only a crude evaluation of economic well-being to either reward or punish the incumbents accordingly. In contrast to voting on ideological proximity considerations, the conventional wisdom has it that the economic voter's task is considerably simpler. While a proximity voter would need to seek information about each party's policy positions and then exert the cognitive effort to measure up party positions to his own, the economic voter casts a ballot either for or against the incumbent based on one simple piece of information – the state of the economy. Clarke (2009, p. 49) aptly depicts this perspective: 'Another way for voters to cope with the complexity of the choices they are being asked to make is to focus on the past rather than the future. This means that they will judge a governing party primarily by its record rather than by its promises.'

While Clarke depicts the economic vote as requiring little information on the part of voters, many others have challenged the notion that economic voting is effortless. A string of articles have made the case for voters' information deficiencies and their limited cognitive capacities to attribute policy outputs to incumbents (Achen and Bartels 2004; De Vries and Giger 2014; Fortunato and Stevenson 2013; Gomez and Wilson 2001, 2006; Hellwig and Marinova 2015). In a study exploring Americans' knowledge of economic performance prior to the 2012 elections, Hellwig and Marinova (2015) show that voters were largely misinformed when requested to provide assessments of important aspects of economic performance – namely, economic growth, inflation, unemployment and the budget deficit. In a large comparative study, De Vries and Giger demonstrate that it is mostly the highly sophisticated citizens who cast an economic vote. Achen and Bartels (2004) and Gomez and Wilson (2001; 2006) find that many voters struggle to attribute responsibility for policy outcomes due to information deficiencies or limited capacity to process information. It would seem then that the economic vote does rest on acquiring a certain amount of information and that doing so is not effortless.

Another piece of evidence that may put a wrinkle in the low-information rationality of the economic vote is its limited span. The extant literature has documented considerable variation across elections in voters' ability to cast a ballot on economic grounds. The variation has been attributed to cross-national institutional differences in the ability of voters to attribute responsibility correctly for the state of the economy; institutions can clarify or obscure to voters which political actors are responsible for economic conditions (Paldam 1991, p. 26; for recent reviews, see Lewis-Beck and Stegmeier 2013; Healy and Malhotra 2013). Powell and Whitten (1993) first showed that retrospective voting is fortified when majority governments are in power and opposition parties have few power-sharing mechanisms. The findings of their widely cited study have been supported in subsequent research.[2] Scholars have since added a number of contextual indicators to the list of institutional variables which 'clarify' responsibility for policy outputs: the availability of viable replacements of the incumbent, length of time the incumbent spent in office, the ideological cohesion of coalition governments and others (e.g., Anderson 2000, Bengtsson 2004, Nadeau *et al.* 2002).[3] Hence, the extent to which voters rely on economic considerations varies widely and is contingent on the electoral and institutional complexity of the choices they are asked to make.

It is important to emphasise that the literature thus far has attributed the weak and inconsistent rates of economic voting to voters' shortfalls while upholding the economic vote as a universally sound strategy of electoral decision-making. Voters' informational shortfalls, skewed perceptions of economic performance and displayed difficulty in attributing responsibility are some of the oft-cited reasons for the inconsistent impact of the economy on the vote. The extant literature has assumed that when voters do not cast an economic vote, it is because they are not *able* to do so. The implicit assumption underpinning this body of work is that economic voting is a universally optimal strategy of electing competent policy makers.

The argument developed in the following section parts ways with the received wisdom in directly challenging the unstated assumption that economic voting is always desirable. It highlights one scenario – party instability – when voters may intentionally neglect, or at least give less weight to, information on economic performance. I argue that doing so is not a sign of cognitive limitation on voters' part; it is reasoned decision-making that can bring about the election of competent policy makers and incentivise good management of the national economy.

Judging the competence of unstable parties: micro-mechanisms

Is economic voting always *a viable strategy* of electing competent politicians?[4] Even if we assume that voters' economic assessments are accurate and responsibility

---

2. See Anderson 2000; Van der Brug *et al.* 2007; Lewis-Beck and Mitchell 1993; Nadeau *et al.* 2002; Norpoth 2002; Powell 2000; Whitten and Palmer 1999.

3. Within the frame of 'clarity of responsibility', a strand of research has added features of the electoral context to the institutions that moderate the rate of retrospective voting. Anderson (2000) and Bengtsson (2004) show that fragmented party systems, operationalised as elections with a large effective number of electoral parties (ENEP), make it more difficult for voters to identify a clear alternative to the incumbent government. A great many opposition parties introduce uncertainty about the shape of a future government as the likely replacements of the incumbent are not as easily predictable. Consequently, voters are less likely to throw the incumbents out of office for poor performance, and retrospective voting and accountability are undermined. Both Anderson (2000) and Bengtsson (2004) find stronger retrospective voting in elections with low ENEP. Hellwig (2011) explores further the relationship between party systems and the ability of voters to sanction incumbents for past performance. Citizens were more likely to vote retrospectively when the positions of parties were more polarised and thus voters had clearer and more diverse policy offerings.

4. Extant literature has not dealt with this question head-on. Indeed we could argue that the sheer amount of research conducted on the contingencies of economic retrospective voting serves to validate it as a viable decision-making rule.

for the economy can be clearly attributed to the incumbent, is economic voting always a reasonable voting strategy to elect a competent future government? In this section, I argue that economic voting may not be an optimal strategy of selecting competent policy makers when parties change between elections. The stability of the electoral choice set presented to voters conditions the viability of economic voting as a decision-making rule.[5] Information on changes in party organisation is essential to shaping voter assessment of parties' governing capacities and should therefore form a central part of economic voting theory. Party instability challenges the universal desirability of economic voting across elections.

The central premise of my argument is that voting – even economic voting – is always prospective in nature.[6] While retrospective voting is based on evaluations of past performance, the vote is always about which party will govern in the future (cf. Kedar 2009). Downs seems to have been aware of this when he wrote, 'it is more rational for him to ground his voting decision on current events than purely on future ones' (1957: p. 40; cf. Clarke 2009). Following from this premise, retrospective economic evaluations become just *a single* piece of information that shapes voters' assessments of competing parties' competences to govern in the future.[7] Not only is information on the economy not effortless to obtain, but it is arguably insufficient to judge the competence of incumbent policy makers. A crucial part of the voters' calculus – and one that has not been probed thus far – includes an assessment of the extent to which past performance is a reasonably good predictor of parties' continued performance and governing competence. Hence, the question I raise here is the following: Are there conditions under which voters may be reluctant to judge governing competence based on past economic performance? I begin by examining the micro foundations of the economic vote and the implications of instability in parties for judging governing competence.

As the basis of sanctioning incumbent for past performance, voters ought to be able to (1) identify the incumbents; (2) judge their competence by, in part, assessing economic performance while in government; and (3) in the case of a negative assessment of the incumbent, select a viable replacement from the opposition.[8] To understand how voters sanction incumbents in elections with unstable parties, we need to understand first the repercussions of party instability for voters' ability to

---

5. See also Hellwig (2012) and Dalton and McAllister (2015) who trace the effects of parties' position switching on electoral accountability. Further, Bækgaard and Jensen (2012) and Somer-Topcu (2009) argue that parties may have incentives to change the electoral choice set when it comes to policy offering.

6. This chapter thus invokes the competency theory of economic voting rather than the accountability theory. In the former, voters use information on the economy to select competent politicians. In the latter, they use economic information to punish or reward politicians in order to incentivise their future effort. For a discussion on these two theories, see Duch and Stevenson (2008).

7. Just as a party's history of change introduces uncertainty about its policymaking in a following government (Chapter Five), so does a party's record in office carry information about its competence in the future. For a critique of models of retrospective voting for failing to incorporate considerations about the future shape of government, see Maravall (2006).

8. In the section below, I refer to these as micro-mechanisms.

identify, assess and replace incumbent governments. Party instability potentially affects the economic vote at each of these three stages. Its effect on voters' ability to tell incumbents apart and to select replacements from the opposition (points (1) and (3)) closely parallel the logic of institutional clarity in responsibility and the complexity of the party and electoral systems reviewed above. Similarly to coalition governments, party instability can obscure responsibility for economic performance by making it more difficult for voters to identify incumbents who have transformed in the course of the electoral campaign. In line with the logic of Anderson's (2000) analysis of high ENEP, party instability can make it harder for voters to select a viable replacement from the opposition when challengers are new or have recently transformed. With respect to (1) and (3), party instability may be regarded as one of many factors that affect voters' ability to attribute responsibility and select replacements to the incumbent.

Where party instability is a game-changer is in judging the competences of incumbent parties (2). A transformation in a party's organisation gives voters reason to believe that past performance is no longer an apt predictor of governing competence and thus renders economic retrospective voting a suboptimal decision-making strategy. My argument parts ways with the extant literature; the latter is largely preoccupied with identifying the conditions under which the economic vote is fortified but nonetheless upholds economic voting as universally desirable. I elaborate on each of these claims in turn.

First, let us examine the impact on party change on voters' ability to identify incumbents (1) and elect viable challengers (3). In order to cast a ballot based on retrospective evaluations of the incumbents' performance, voters would first need to identify the incumbent party or parties. This may be a relatively simple task when parties run for reelection unchanged but a cognitively demanding one when incumbent parties transform between elections. Take as an example the 1996 parliamentary election in Romania where the incumbent party underwent considerable change between the 1992 and 1996 elections. The ruling Democratic National Salvation Front not only changed its name to the Romanian Party of Social Democracy (PSDR), but it also merged with three smaller parties which did not form part of the ruling coalition (the Socialist Democratic Party of Romania, the Cooperative Party, and the Republican Party). Electoral spaces characterised by unstable party organisations place higher cognitive demands on voters than those of relative party stability (*see* Chapter Two). We can thus expect that identifying the incumbent and challenger parties is likely to be more taxing when parties undergo organisational discontinuities than when they remain stable. Voters who are unable to identify the incumbent and opposition on the ballot are in turn less likely to sanction the incumbents correctly for their performance in office, resulting in lower rates of economic voting.

In addition to identifying the incumbent(s), voters need to be able to assess the challenger parties if – in the case of a negative assessment of economic performance – they wish to select a viable replacement from the opposition (3). As Anderson (2000) has shown, despite negative assessments of economic performance, voters are much less likely to sanction the incumbent when no viable opposition parties run for election. The opposition may be easily identified and evaluated when it consists of a handful of long-standing, stable parties that are familiar to voters. With high instability in challenger parties, however, it becomes increasingly difficult for voters to identify the opposition and assess its viability. Akin to a high number of ENEPs in a given election, party instability poses a challenge to economic voting when it comes to evaluating opposition parties. In elections where challenger parties undergo repeated transformation or when the opposition is comprised of many new parties, it likely becomes difficult for voters to assess the viability of each alternative on the ballot. Following the results from Anderson (2000), we can expect voters to be more likely to turn away from new and transformed opposition candidacies and to cast a ballot for the incumbent *despite* having evaluated incumbents' performance in office *un*favourably.

Whereas party instability renders the identification of incumbency status and the evaluation of challengers more difficult, it makes the assessment of governing competence based on retrospective information unsound (2). In the classical economic voting model, voters should judge the competence of parties by relying on their knowledge of parties' past record of governance. Having a general idea of parties' governing competence helps voters form expectations about the future trajectories of parties; if a party has a favourable record in office, then voters may reasonably expect that it continue performing well, and vice versa. However, instability interrupts the continuity of party organisations and thereby introduces uncertainty about their subsequent performance trajectories. A split within a party or a merger with another party is likely to alter considerably the competences of incumbents. As parties change between electoral cycles, voters will have reasons to doubt that their prior knowledge would continue to hold as a reasonable predictor of subsequent performance. Retrospective voting is no longer as optimal – or straightforward – of a voting strategy as it is in elections with long-standing, stable parties.

After a party change, reasoned voters would no longer use economic retrospections as their sole evaluation criterion of governing competence but would weigh these evaluations against the uncertainty introduced by party instability. How will they do so? Will voters weigh party change as positive or negative when it comes to judging competence? Given the evidence that voters generally shy away from unstable parties in order to minimise risk and uncertainty (*see* Chapter Five), it is likely that voters also err on the safe side when it comes to electing policymakers based on their competence. Following the logic of the third mechanism, a positive evaluation of the economy would not necessarily translate into a vote for the incumbent when parties are in flux; voters are likely to shy away from well-performing incumbents when those incumbents have changed. In contrast, if voters are reasoned decision-makers, a negative evaluation of the economy should *not* translate into a vote for the incumbent when parties are in flux.[9] I develop these expectations in the following section.

---

9. This would spell out the logic of mechanism (2).

Preliminary expectations

Taken together, these arguments have empirical implications for the extent to which voters apply economic voting as a decision-making strategy at the individual level and for the extent to which electoral accountability is fulfilled at the national level. At the micro level, we can expect higher party instability to bring about lower rates of economic retrospective voting (Expectation 1). As party instability rises, voters will be less likely to decide based on their retrospective evaluations of the economy; hence, we would observe a weakening relationship between voters' economic retrospections and vote for the incumbent. We can extend this logic to aggregate election results. Due to voters' propensity to give lower weight to economic considerations as party instability rises, we will likely observe that macroeconomic performance becomes a weaker predictor of the electoral fortunes of incumbents (Expectation 2).

While all three micro-mechanisms specified above have the same observable implication (weaker economic voting as party instability increases in Expectation 1), they supply fundamentally different sets of logic for the same empirical relationship. Mechanisms (1) and (3) suggest that voters cast an economic vote at lower rates because they are unable to grapple with the electoral complexity generated by party change. Voters are either unable to tell incumbents apart from challengers, or they are unable to assess the viability of challenger parties and thus default to the incumbent. In contrast, mechanism (2) suggests that voters give lower weight to economic evaluations because the latter carry limited information about the competence of transformed parties. In mechanism (2), the complexity generated by instability informs, rather than hazes, voter decision-making processes. The relationships between evaluations of the economy and the vote can help distill between these conflicting sets of logic.

Following this reasoning, we will observe starkly different patterns in the data which can help us distinguish between the mechanisms at work. If mechanism (1) is at work, voters are likely to err on both sides: selecting an incumbent when their assessment of the economy is poor and selecting challengers when their assessment of the economy is positive. If lower rates of economic voting are due to voters' inability to tell incumbents apart from challengers, we will likely observe both of these patterns in the data. If mechanism (3) is at work, voters are likely to err on the side of selecting incumbents *despite* negative evaluations of the economy. If lower rates of economic voting are due to voters' inability to identify viable challengers, then we will observe voters choosing incumbents not by choice but by default. Finally, if mechanism (2) is at work, cautious voters' will err on the side of challengers *despite* favourable evaluations of economic performance. If lower rates of economic voting are due to voters weighing economic information against the uncertainty of party change, then well-performing incumbents will be elected at lower rates.

Testing these expectations promises to contribute to our understanding of accountability in elections by moving past the institutional conditions which facilitate or hinder the rate of economic voting across elections. Thus far the extant literature has not questioned the degree to which economic voting is an optimal decision-making strategy in all elections. I have argued that if the goal is to elect competent policy makers, then voters would be misguided if they were to rely on retrospective economic evaluations alone as parties transform. If micro-mechanism (2) receives empirical support, the implication would be that the economic vote is not a strategy suitable to all elections; the logic of economic voting would rather be contingent on whether parties remain unchanged between electoral cycles and the degree to which their past performance can serve as an approximation of their governing capacity.

Data and method of analysis

Understanding how changes in electoral spaces influence the decision-making of voters calls for a comparative analysis. The empirical implications of the hypotheses above will manifest at the micro and macro levels of analysis. To test Expectation 1, I use CSES survey data on vote choice and evaluation of government performance along with election-level data on instability. To test Expectation 2, I use macro-level data on electoral performance of the incumbent, national economic performance, political institutions and election-level party instability. The data and methods for these two sets of analyses are discussed below.

For the micro-level analyses, the dependent variable is binary, coded 1 if the respondent cast a ballot for the incumbent and 0 if she cast a ballot for the opposition. The principal independent variable of interest is respondents' *evaluations of government performance* in office. Respondents were asked, 'Now thinking about the performance of the government in general, how good or bad a job do you think the government has done over the past [NUMBER] years? Has it done a very good job (4)? A good job (3)? A bad job (2)? A very bad job (1)?'[10]

In addition, a number of individual and contextual control variables are included in the analysis. To control for ideological differences between respondents and the incumbent, I measure the left-right *ideological distance* between the respondent and the incumbent as the absolute difference between (1) respondents' self-reported left-right placement and (2) the placement of the prime minister's party on the left-right ideological continuum by national political experts. Increasing left-right distance between voters and the incumbent should be associated with a declining probability of voting for the incumbent. *Age*, *gender* and *education* are included as control variables. In order to control for institutional confounding factors, I include a variable for *clarity of responsibility* at the election level of analysis (Tavits 2007). Clarity of responsibility is an index of four indicators that have been previously linked to higher rates of economic retrospective voting: the majority status of government, cabinet duration, opposition influence and the

---

10. Due to a large number of missing values for this variable in Module 2 of the CSES, I combined evaluation of general performance with performance assessment on the most important issue (as identified by the respondent in a previous question). This contributed 26,832 additional observations to the data set.

effective number of parties. The four measures are standardised, and overall clarity varies between -10.8 and 13.3, where the United Kingdom scores the highest while clarity is lowest in Italy and Belgium.[11]

I analyse the data using a mixed-effects logit model with individuals nested in elections. Formally we can express the probability of voting for the incumbent as $logit[Pr(Incumbent_i = 1) | X_{ij}\zeta_j] = \beta_0 + \beta_1 E_i + \beta_2 EIP_j + \beta 3 E_j EIP_j + \gamma X_{ij} + \zeta_j$, where E_i is the evaluation of government performance of respondent i, EIP_j is party instability in election j, X_{ij} is a vector of individual and election-specific control variables, γ is a vector of slopes, and δ_j constitutes election-specific factors not accounted for by the covariates that may otherwise affect the likelihood of voting for the incumbent (Rabe-Hesketh and Skrondal 2008; Raudenbush and Bryk 2002). The mixed-effects logistic regression is fitted via maximum likelihood estimation.

Of interest is the sign on the interaction coefficient β_3. A negative sign would offer evidence that, as party instability rises, incumbent parties are penalised at lower rates for poor performance, and vice versa, incumbents are rewarded at lower rates for satisfactory performance. Voters would be increasingly less likely to vote based solely on their retrospective performance evaluations as party instability rises. A negative sign would thus offer evidence in support of Expectation 1. In addition to the main interaction, I control at the micro level for the clarity of responsibility afforded by institutions at the election level. I test for an interaction between EIP_j and E_i under low and high institutional clarity of responsibility.

To test the macro-level implications of party instability for electoral accountability, I use national-level election and economic data kindly provided by Samuels and Hellwig (2010). Their data spans through the year 2004, and overall 100 parliamentary elections from twenty-five European countries overlapped with the data collected on party instability (*see* Chapter Three). The dependent variable in the macro-level analysis is *incumbent vote share*, or the per centage of the vote received by the incumbent party. If the incumbent performed poorly, we expect its share of the vote to shrink, and vice versa. This would uphold electoral accountability. The incumbent party is coded in two ways: as the party with the largest seat share in the past election (legislative incumbent party) and as the party of the president (executive incumbent party).

To test Expectation 2 at the macro level of analysis, I assess the degree of electoral accountability in elections. I test the effect of economic performance, operationalised as economic growth over the year prior to the election, on the electoral success of the incumbent in election j. The models fitted may be expressed as *Incumbent Vote Share$_j$* $= \beta_0 + \beta_1 Growth_j + \gamma X_j + \varepsilon$, where β_1 is the effect of economic growth on the electoral success of the incumbent, Xj is a vector of control variables, γ is a vector of slopes, and is the error.

Economic growth is operationalised as the annual per centage change in per capita GDP. I include a number of control variables: the *age of democracy* and the

---

11. I have rescaled Tavits' original index by multiplying the original scores by ten in order to compare more easily to coefficients to EIP.

incumbent's vote share in the previous election. The latter is necessary to assess the degree to which incumbents are punished for economic performance given their past electoral performance as a baseline. Following Samuels and Hellwig (2010), to estimate the conditioning effects of clarity of institutional responsibility and party instability on the process of electoral accountability, I model the effects of economic performance on incumbent success using interactive modelling techniques. The interactive modelling techniques allow me to examine β_1 under varying levels of party instability and clarity of institutional responsibility. I perform a post-estimation analysis to obtain conditional coefficients and their standard errors (Kam and Franzese 2007). If electoral accountability works well, we expect to see a positive sign on β_1.

To account for potential differences in democratic outcomes between new and mature democracies, I control for the *age of democracy*. As the effect of democratic longevity may decline over time, I include its square term (cf. Samuels and Hellwig 2010). To estimate clarity of responsibility, I rely on data from Tavits (2007). Furthermore, I control for levels of *democratic development* which is measured by a multiplicative index of the number of years since the first democratic election and the reversed Freedom House score of political rights (a higher score denotes a higher level of democratic development). The models are estimated using OLS with Huber-White robust standard errors clustered by country. I convey the key information with the coefficient on economic growth.

Empirical findings

Overall the results offer evidence of a strong, negative effect of party instability on retrospective voting: the higher party instability is in an election, the less likely voters are to decide based on their evaluations of incumbents' past performance in office (Expectation 1). The results are consistent with the reasoned decision-making described in mechanism (2). As elections become increasingly unstable, voters give lower weight to economic considerations: voters are less likely to re-elect incumbents despite positive evaluations of the economy but are no more likely to elect incumbents whose performance they judge to be subpar. In other words, parties of poor economic records are not successful in throwing dust in voters' eyes by initiating party instability. The macro-level results are consistent with the findings at the micro level. Party instability weakens the relationship between objective macroeconomic performance and the vote share of the incumbent (Expectation 2). I describe the findings below.

Table 6.1 presents results from several model specifications testing Expectation 1. The empirical strategy consists of adding control variables and interaction terms in successive models. Model 1 serves as a baseline for comparison. Model 2 adds controls for the institutional effects. The following two models test the effect of EIP on economic voting in low and high clarity elections. The final model specifies a three-way interaction between performance evaluations, EIP and institutions. Overall party instability weakens the rate of economic retrospective voting (Model 1 joint F-test, $p<0.0001$). The effect of party instability is amplified under institutions affording *high* clarity of responsibility (Model 5 joint F-test, $p<0.001$). The results are discussed in detail below.

A model with individual-level covariates only (not shown) indicates that increasing ideological distance from the prime minister's party decreases the likelihood of voting for the incumbent. Furthermore, more positive evaluations of government performance have a strong effect on vote choice in the expected direction. On average respondents who assess government performance as 'good' or 'very good' are, respectively, six and thirteen times more likely to vote for an incumbent party than are respondents who assess performance as 'very poor'. Performance evaluations are thus modelled as a factor variable to reflect the non-linear effect of evaluations on the vote. The estimated residuals of the null model of incumbent vote choice without predictors (not shown) indicate substantial between-election variation in retrospective voting. This is confirmed by the likelihood ratio test that the random-effects intercept equals zero ($p<0.001$). The between-election predicted probability of casting a vote for the incumbent ranges widely: between 0.16 and 0.77. Given the high between-election variation, I proceed to include election-level covariates.

Estimates from Model 1 offer support for the proposition that voters give retrospective economic evaluations lower weight when parties transform. This proposition is tested with a set of two-way interaction terms between EIP and each category of performance (joint F-test, $p<0.0001$). To interpret the interaction terms, Figure 6.1 plots predicted probabilities of voting for the incumbent for voters who evaluated government performance as 'very good' and 'very poor', respectively.[12] As party instability rises, we observe shrinking differences in predicted probabilities for the two groups. In a stable election, those who hold positive evaluations of government performance are four times more likely to vote for an incumbent party; when EIP reaches five party changes, the former are only three times as likely to vote for the incumbent. Voters who held government performance in high esteem were increasingly likely to vote against their evaluations as party instability rose. In such elections, we observe the opposite of what theories of economic voting dictate: performance evaluations become less central to electoral decision-making.

The predicted probabilities in Figure 6.1 hint at the micro-mechanism at work. The shrinking differences between the two sets of voters are due to those voters who evaluated performance as 'very good' becoming less likely to cast a ballot based on their evaluations. In contrast, voters who evaluated performance as 'very poor' were no more likely to vote for the incumbent as party instability rose. Hence the former gave lower weight to economic evaluations and higher weight to the uncertainty triggered by party instability. This is consistent with the empirical results in Chapter Five where voters were shown to be generally less likely to vote for parties that had undergone organisational change. In contrast, when economic performance is evaluated poorly, party instability can do little to reassure voters

---

12. Age and ideological distance are set to the sample mean. Male and education are set to zero.

Figure 6.1: Predicted probability of economic voting by electoral instability in parties

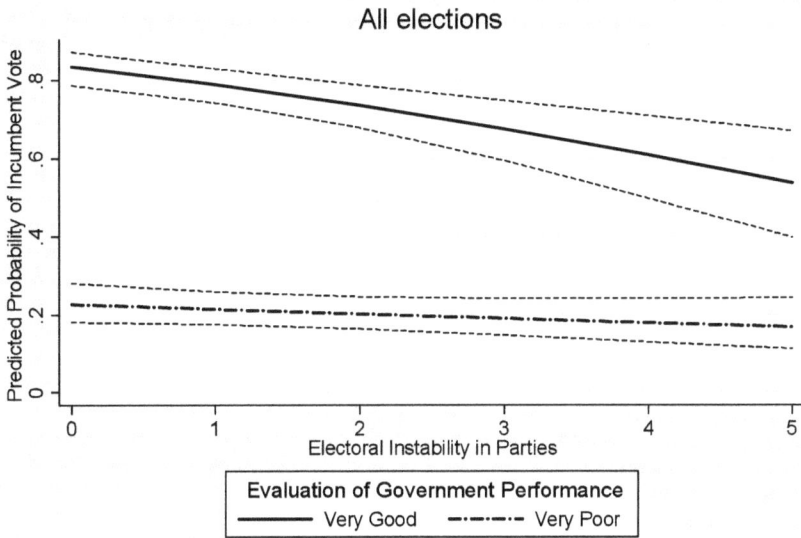

All elections

Note: Predicted probabilities are based on Model 1 in Table 1. 95 per cent confidence intervals reported.

of incumbents' governing capacity. It is therefore unlikely that parties succeed in sweeping a poor record of governance under the rug by initiating organisational change. These patterns are consistent with the reasoned decision-making described in micro-mechanism (2).

The next set of models tests these effects further under different institutional settings. Figure 6.2 plots the predicted probabilities of incumbent voting in elections of low and high clarity of responsibility, respectively. The results in Model 1 hold up for low-clarity elections and are amplified in high-clarity elections. As prior research suggests, the sanctioning of incumbents for their performance is much stronger in the latter set of electoral systems. When no parties change in elections, those voters offering positive evaluations of performance are nearly six times more likely to cast a vote for the incumbent than are respondents offering negative evaluations. The comparable figure in low-clarity elections is 2.9. These predicted odds change significantly as instability in parties rises. In low-clarity systems, we see diminishing but statistically significant differences in vote choice as party instability increases. Voters evaluating performance as 'very good' are three times more likely to cast a vote for the incumbent with five party changes (compare to predicted odds of six when EIP is zero). In high-clarity electoral systems, the predicted probabilities for the two sets of voters are not statistically different after EIP passes three party changes in an election. Given the small sample of high-clarity elections, the large confidence intervals are not surprising. The right-hand panel in

Figure 6.2: Predicted probability of economic voting by electoral instability in parties and clarity of institutional responsibility

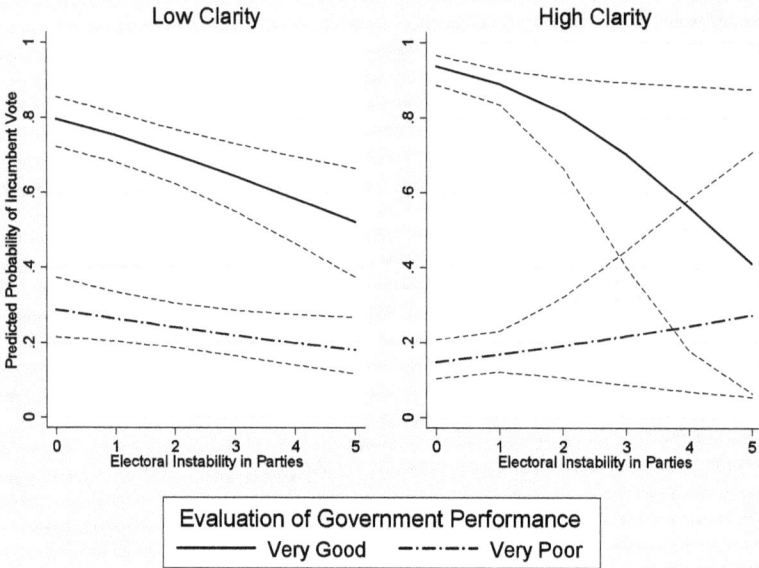

Note: Predicted probabilities are based on Models 3 and 4 in Table 1. 95 per cent confidence intervals reported.

Figure 6.2 should thus be interpreted with caution. The figure illustrates opposite trends for those expressing positive and negative evaluations, respectively. With increasing instability, the former are increasingly less likely to support incumbent candidates while the latter are more likely to do so. Overall, in both low- and high-clarity electoral systems, voters weigh performance evaluations less heavily as parties transform. While clarity of responsibility can amplify the effects of party instability on economic voting, controlling for institutional properties does not do away with the effect of party change.

A set of additional analyses and robustness checks were carried out. First, the hypotheses were tested with an equivalent set of models for vote choice for the prime minister's party. The results are presented in the Appendix (Tables A.7, A.8 and A.9). The coefficients on the interaction terms trend in the same direction but are considerably smaller in magnitude when incumbent vote is operationalised as vote for the executive's party. This suggests that the executive's party continues to be held to accounts even as instability rises. This is not surprising given the higher visibility of the prime minister's party. Second, the hypotheses were tested for electoral instability in incumbent and opposition parties separately. Instability in parties has a disruptive effect on accountability whether it stems from opposition or incumbent parties. The magnitude of the effect is larger for instability originating in the former than in the latter; however, this may be an artefact of the higher number of party changes in opposition parties, and the differences between the effects of opposition party instability and incumbent party instability should be interpreted with caution. Third, the regressions controlled for geographical region, but this did not alter the significance or the magnitude of the findings presented in Table 6.1. Finally, several potential outliers emerged upon examination of the election-level random effects. In Swiss elections, the probability of voting for an incumbent party was unusually high while in Polish elections it was unusually low. In Poland and Norway, we observe on average a negative relationship between performance evaluations and vote for the incumbent. Finally, in Bulgaria-2001 and Poland-2001, levels of party instability were unusually high. The results reported in Table 6.1 were robust to the exclusion of these elections from the sample.

Tables 6.2–6.3 present results from the macro-level analyses testing Expectation 2. If electoral accountability works well, we expect economic growth to be a strong and positive predictor of vote share for the incumbent (operationalised as either the legislative party or executive party). The models presented in Tables 6.2–6.3 compare the relationship between economic outcomes and the vote for the incumbent under varying levels of party instability and clarity of responsibility. Note that the size of all coefficients is low due to the inclusion of a lag variable. We can thus interpret these differences as changes with respect to baseline support for incumbents in the previous election cycle. The first row in each table presents estimates of the accountability coefficient in contexts of low (left) and high (right) instability in parties.[13] In elections of low instability, incumbents are rewarded by 0.76 per centage points for a unit change in economic growth. In elections of high instability, however, legislative and executive incumbents are rewarded by 0.6 and 1.3 per centage points, respectively, *despite* economic declines. In many close elections in our sample, including Spain-1996, Denmark-2001, Portugal-2002 and Romania-2004, this could spell the difference between electoral success and defeat. Before controlling for institutional context, we see evidence that instability in parties undermines the principles of electoral accountability based on macroeconomic performance.

The following two rows in Tables 6.2–6.3 test the relationship between EIP and electoral accountability under low and high levels of institutional clarity of responsibility (one standard deviation below or above the mean). High clarity of institutional responsibility brings about electoral accountability only when party instability is low. In high-clarity low-EIP contexts, accountability works well in that legislative parties are rewarded by a per centage increase in their vote share ($p<0.01$). However, when EIP is high, high clarity does not bring about electoral accountability; with just three party changes, high institutional clarity of responsibility no longer exerts a positive effect on electoral accountability. This suggests that high clarity of institutional responsibility cannot mitigate the negative effects of party instability. In low-clarity elections in contrast, the relationship between growth and accountability is negative or not statistically different from

---

13. Low EIP is set to 0, and high EIP is set to 3. This represents the 25th and 75th per centiles in the distribution of EIP.

Table 6.1: Mixed-effects logistic model of incumbent vote

	All elections: EIP (1)	All elections: EIP and clarity (2)	Low-clarity elections (3)	High-clarity elections (4)	All elections: Full spec. (5)
Age	0.006***	0.007***	0.004***	0.012***	0.007***
	0.0007	0.0007	0.0008	0.0013	0.0007
Male	−0.032	−0.034	−0.062*	0.038	−0.034
	0.0225	0.0226	0.0265	0.0429	0.0226
University education	−0.004	−0.002	0.052	−0.136*	−0.003
	0.0287	0.0289	0.0339	0.0548	0.0289
Ideological distance	−0.048***	−0.048***	−0.036***	−0.081***	−0.048***
	0.0014	0.0014	0.0016	0.0031	0.0014
Electoral instability (EIP)	−0.075	−0.187**	−0.130*	0.181	−0.125
	0.0550	0.0645	0.0635	0.1341	0.1362
Performance evaluation					
Very poor	(base)	(base)	(base)	(base)	(base)
Poor	0.614***	0.678***	0.313***	0.990***	0.614***
	0.0439	0.0457	0.0564	0.0799	0.0439
Good	1.931***	2.050***	1.491***	2.603***	1.931***
	0.0473	0.0492	0.0594	0.0888	0.0473
Very good	2.841***	3.206***	2.267***	4.438***	2.841***
	0.0842	0.0956	0.0954	0.2726	0.0842
Performance x EIP					
Very poor x EIP	(base)	(base)	(base)	(base)	(base)
Poor x EIP	−0.028	0.066***	0.019	−0.139*	0.014
	0.0153	0.0179	0.0165	0.0697	0.0329
Good x EIP	−0.115***	0.095***	−0.044*	−0.214**	0.154***
	0.0208	0.0231	0.0220	0.0790	0.0399
Very good x EIP	−0.219***	0.026	−0.133**	−0.765***	−0.073
	0.0425	0.0420	0.0425	0.2020	0.0836

Table 6.1 (*continued*)

	All elections: EIP (1)	All elections: EIP and clarity (2)	Low-clarity elections (3)	High-clarity elections (4)	All elections: Full spec. (5)
Performance x Clarity					
Very poor x Clarity		−0.127*** 0.0291			−0.139*** 0.0336
Poor x Clarity		−0.022 0.0284			−0.021 0.0322
Good x Clarity		0.061* 0.0285			0.040 0.0324
Very good x Clarity		0.150*** 0.0329			0.174*** 0.0428
Performance x EIP x Clarity					
Very poor x EIP x Clarity					0.011 0.0177
Poor x EIP x Clarity					0.001 0.0173
Good x EIP x Clarity					0.022 0.0175
Very good x EIP x Clarity					−0.010 0.0223
Constant	−1.108*** 0.1497	−1.200*** 0.1485	−0.781*** 0.2034	−1.610*** 0.2189	−1.228*** 0.1539
Variance components					
Intercept	0.778*** 0.086	0.767*** 0.085	0.829*** 0.114	0.626*** 0.117	0.768*** 0.085
Ni / Nj	42,173/ 42	42,173/42	29,357/ 27	12,816/ 15	42,173/ 42

Note: Table 1 reports coefficient estimates from a mixed-effects logistic regression. The dependent variable is incumbent vote (coded 1 if the respondent indicated voting for an incumbent party). Models 3 and 4 partition the sample into elections with low (below 0) and high clarity of responsibility (above 0). *$p < 0.05$, **$p < 0.01$, ***$p < 0.001$

Table 6.2: Modelling accountability for the economy: vote for the incumbent legislative party

Clarity of resp.	Party Instability	
	Low	High
All	0.79†	−0.59†
Low	−0.12	−.86†
High	1.13**	0.36

Note: All models estimated with robust standard errors clustered by country. The table reports estimates for β from estimating *Incumbent Vote* $= \alpha + \beta*Economy + \gamma_1*AgeDem + \gamma_2*AgeDem^2 + \gamma_3*Previous\ Vote + \varepsilon$ with β conditioned on party instability and clarity of responsibility. Models estimated with OLS. ***$p < 0.001$, **$p < 0.01$, *$p < 0.05$, †$p < 0.1$. N=93 elections.

Table 6.3: Modelling accountability for the economy: vote for the incumbent executive party

Clarity of resp.	Party Instability	
	Low	High
All	0.09	−1.26**
Low	−0.91*	−1.86***
High	0.43	−0.59

Note: All models estimated with robust standard errors clustered by country. The table reports estimates for β from estimating *Incumbent Vote* $= \alpha + \beta*Economy + \gamma_1*AgeDem + \gamma_2*AgeDem^2 + \gamma_3*Previous\ Vote + \varepsilon$ with β conditioned on party instability and clarity of responsibility. Models estimated with OLS. ***$p < 0.001$, **$p < 0.01$, *$p < 0.05$, †$p < 0.1$. N=91 elections.

zero. High party instability amplifies this effect. Together, these findings suggest that low clarity of responsibility is not sufficient for electoral accountability to function well. High levels of party instability undermine electoral accountability in elections, and this effect is stronger when party instability also takes place in low-clarity contexts. The concluding section offers some implications of these findings.

Conclusions

This chapter posed the following questions: Is information on the state of the economy sufficient to cast an economic vote as parties transform? The theoretical discussion and empirical results answer in the negative. I have argued that changes in party organisations make it *less rational* on the part of voters to rely on retrospective economic evaluations when casting a ballot for the incumbent. This is because party instability comes head-to-head with the logic of economic voting. When voters sanction incumbents based on the economy, it is under the assumption that past performance is a good predictor of incumbents' future governing capacity. Party instability interrupts the continuity of the organisation and adds considerable uncertainty about the extent to which past performance is a good predictor of governance in the future. Party instability thus challenges one of the main assumptions on which economic voting rests. As a consequence, reasoned voters ought to rely on retrospective economic evaluations more sparingly as parties transform. This is indeed what the empirical results suggest. High levels of party instability considerably reduce the association between voters' positive evaluations of the economy and their propensity to re-elect incumbents. The magnitude of the change is considerable – the predicted odds of an economic vote are twice as likely when parties are stable – and the relationship is robust to various model specifications.

What are the implications of these findings electoral accountability and political representation? In the case of high party instability, lower rates of economic voting spell good news for electoral accountability and political representation. To my knowledge, this is the first study that does *not* ring the alarm bell on weak economic voting. Where party instability is high, I have argued that economic retrospections alone would not offer voters a good sense of parties' governing capacities after the election. Voters need to take into account information on party changes and assess how well past performance predicts governing competence after parties have transformed. I would argue that when voters do not rely on strict retrospective economic evaluations, they are likely making a sound decision. My argument challenges the well-entrenched belief that economic voting should be upheld across elections. Like other scholars (Kedar 2009; Maravall 2006), I have developed my argument on the premise that voting is ultimately about who will govern in the future; economic voting is about judging the governing capacities of competing parties. Reward incumbents for reward's sake would not necessarily bring about the election of competent policy makers. Voters take into account economic performance along with other factors that shape the governing capacity of parties, including organisational changes. That, I would argue, is a good thing.

The results of this chapter also weigh in on the low-information rationality debate behind economic voting. Is the economic vote ultimately a low-information strategy as scholars have long upheld it to be (Key 1966; Fiorina 1981)? Perhaps the answer to this question is always relative; the economic vote may require less information than, say, ideological voting, and yet more information than, say, candidate liking. The results from this chapter shed some new light on this question but do not answer it definitively. Voters seem capable of weighing economic considerations against other relevant factors even in complex electoral spaces. While rates of economic voting are lower under unstable parties, the spirit of economic voting is not violated. Voters' decision to give lower weight to retrospective evaluations is consistent with the logic of electing competent policy makers. Yet, economic voting does not serve voters as an adaptive, low-information strategy. Clearly, we cannot assume greater reliance on economic considerations simply on account of voters' lower knowledge of transforming parties' policy positions (Chapter Four). Whatever the final verdict on the low-information rationality of economic voting, this chapter makes clear that when it comes to complex election environments, voters do not resort to economic considerations as a way out.

Chapter Seven

Conclusion: A New Look at Old Theories

Two central questions motivated this research: How do voters adapt to the complexity of electoral information? What are the implications of voters' coping mechanisms for the practice of representative democracy? I have focused on one case of complexity where the electoral alternatives are not fixed over time and where parties emerge, fuse, split and die off. Such an electoral landscape is markedly different from that assumed in extant research, and its properties have previously not been studied in their own right. The extant literature on political behaviour has been built on the assumption that the alternatives on the ballot are well defined and continuous over time. Instability in party organisations shakes this assumption with important consequences for the quality of voters' information environments and the extent to and ways in which voters acquire and process electoral information.

I have argued that instability in party organisations increases the complexity of voters' information environments. The emergence of new parties and changes in existing ones increase the sheer amount of new information that voters need to acquire. Instability also makes it more difficult for voters to attribute cues to parties as the sources of information are less well known and continuously changing. The greater amount of information and the lower effectiveness with which it is communicated contribute to higher costs in acquiring electoral information. As a consequence, party instability puts a strain on voter information seeking. Erratic elections with many transformed parties compel significant cognitive effort on the part of voters as party cues are costlier to pay attention to and process. In Chapter Four, I show that party instability generally contributes to lower levels of familiarity with parties' policy positions. I find that even the well-educated voter is not spared in highly complex elections; rather than enabling voters to cope with the higher levels of complexity triggered by party instability, education serves as an advantage *only when* the information environment lends itself to information acquisition.

How do voters cope when they dispose of little information on parties' policy positions? Drawing on dual-processing theories of cognitive decision-making, I lay out a number of low-information heuristics that voters potentially use to discern and decide between parties: ideological extremism, leader charisma, a party's history of change and the state of the economy. The findings in Chapters Five and Six illustrate that voters rely on a unique set of decision-making heuristics to cope with the information shortfalls triggered by party instability. First, due to lower levels of familiarity with transformed parties' policy stances, voters relied on *diffuse* and less cognitively taxing perceptions of party positions (namely, the direction and intensity of policy stances) to choose between competing actors. Second, voters were considerably more likely to be swayed by their gut feelings towards party leaders when voting for new and splinter parties, suggesting an elevated effect of leader charisma in the absence of clear policy positions. Third, when parties underwent changes between elections, voters used instability as a cue in and of itself, thus minimising uncertainty by shunning lesser known initiatives on the ballot. Finally, voters were considerably less likely to rely on their evaluations of economic performance when casting a ballot. As argued in Chapter Six, the viability of economic evaluations in predicting parties' future governing capacity is conditional on the organisational continuity of parties. Together the results offer considerable evidence that voters adapt to unstable parties with a unique set of decision-making rules.

In the remainder of this chapter I explore the implications of these findings for extant theories of political behaviour. I raise the following questions: Do the low-information heuristics used contribute to good decision-making outcomes? In other words, are voters in some ways 'tricked' or confused by the electoral manoeuvring of party organisations? Does the vote in complex information environments measure up to the standards upheld in normative theories of electoral representation? What are the implications of party instability for citizen-elite linkages and substantive representation? Far from raising red flags, I argue that the evidence of adaptive heuristics suggests that voters are versatile and ingenious decision-makers; they adapt to informational complexity with a set of cognitively less costly heuristics uniquely suited to the challenges they face. In sharp contrast to normative theories of political behaviour, I argue that the implications of voters' decision-making mechanisms in complex elections are far from detrimental to representative democracy and, in some cases, contribute to more desirable electoral outcomes in the context of party change. Approaching electoral decision-making from the viewpoint of political parties shaping the information environment opens the door to a more nuanced and context-focused approach to political behaviour. I examine the advantages to a bottom-up approach to informational heuristics and draw parallels with and contrasts to the dominant approach. I conclude by offering paths for future research on the linkages of party and voter behaviour.

Voting for unstable parties: rational processes, reasoned outcomes

Are complex information environments suitable to rational and reasoned decision-making? This is one of the important questions preoccupying political psychologists today (Carmines and D'Amico 2015). On one hand, we are interested in the rationality or efficiency of decision-making (i.e., the process). On the other hand, we are also interested in the quality of electoral outcomes, or how reasoned voters' decisions are (i.e., the outcome). The initial findings of this book put a question mark over the compatibility of highly complex information contexts and reasoned decision-making outcomes. The complexity of elections contributes to lower levels of knowledge about party positions; such information is in turn considered critical to reasoned vote choice. A well-informed voters is more likely to turn out in elections and vote according to his or her preferences (e.g., Andersen *et al.* 2005; Gomez and Wilson 2001; Lau and Redlawsk 2001; Marquis 2010). Based on past research linking political knowledge to desirable electoral outcomes, party instability spells bad news for reasoned electoral choice. At first glance, it may thus seem that party instability is a destabilising force that precludes informed decision-making and leads to inferior electoral outcomes.

The remainder of empirical findings in this book contradicts this initial conclusion. For one, lower levels of familiarity with party positions do not altogether preclude policy-based voting. Rather than barring the use of political ideology in electoral decision-making, voters adapt to lower information by using political ideology in a distinctly different way. Voters who select new or transformed parties tend to rely on the direction and intensity of these parties' programmatic appeals rather than their exact positions in policy space. Lower levels of political knowledge therefore do not translate into an absolute lack of programmatic voting but instead reshape the ways in which voters piece together party positions and use political ideology as a heuristic. As determining the policy positions of newly formed parties requires considerably more effort on the part of voters, voters pursue the rational, cognitive resource-saving alternative of relying on the direction and intensity of party appeals. The latter type of information is arguably much more accessible in low-information elections than are parties' exact policy stances. As Rabinowitz and MacDonald (1989) argued originally, direction-intensity rules are particularly well suited in elections where the costs of acquiring information are high. As the exact policy positions of newly formed parties are more difficult to determine, voters who seek to make efficient use of their time and cognitive resources may well respond to extreme – yet clear – policy cues. The extreme policy positions of new parties serve as useful cues to voters and thus have an important informational function in and of themselves. We could thus conceive of voters' reliance on direction-intensity rather than proximity rules as rational and efficient use of scarce information on party ideology.

Another example of the efficient and rational use of limited resources in complex elections is the reliance on gut feelings towards party leaders. It is reasonable on the part of voters to look to factors other than the policy stances of parties when party positions cannot be easily told apart (cf. Alvarez 1998). Political personalities are a prime candidate for an alternative decision-making rule when parties are new or newly transformed. Consider that younger parties tend to be less embedded in social cleavages, dispose of weaker organisational structures and have only nascent membership bases (Grofman *et al.* 2000). We could add further that, as newcomers, their policy stances may lack credibility as compared to long-standing parties. As a result, young political formations often run on salient political personalities (Ramonaite 2007; cf. Tverdova 2011). Stronger leader effects in complex elections suggest that voters adapt to the scarcity of policy information by relying on the cues that are readily available – in this case, information on political personalities. Together, the findings from Chapters Five and Six suggest that the decisions of voters embedded in complex elections with unstable parties are rational; they rely on more readily available information (e.g., party leader charisma, the intensity of party positions) and do so efficiently (i.e., minimising cognitive effort and making full use of scarce information).

The natural follow-up question is whether these efficient decision-making rules contribute to good electoral outcomes. Given the scarcity of policy information and given that the use of such information is held to be the single most important ingredient for reasoned vote choice, does reliance on alternative low-information heuristics impede sound electoral choices? The findings of this book answer in the negative. Consider voters' reliance on direction-intensity rules first. When voters decide based on the intensity of party positions, they favour parties with more extreme policy stances. Consequently, the elevated reliance on direction-intensity appeals for new and transformed parties contributes to the electoral success of parties of more extreme ideological positions (cf. Hinich and Munger 1997). Such parties have long preoccupied scholars of electoral politics, but there is evidence that new political formations become driven towards the mainstream once elected into parliament (Flanagan and Dalton 1984; Mudde 1996; Rydgren 2005).[1] In the short run, reliance on direction-intensity appeals contributes to the election of more ideologically extreme parties. However, over the long run the election of such parties into office does not tend to translate into radical politics.

Even more promising are the results suggesting that voters are able to identify correctly risk and uncertainty in elections. Voters generally shy away from newcomers and newly transformed parties. I argue that this speaks well of voters' decision-making capacities and ultimately constitutes good news for political representation. Newcomers carry considerable uncertainty because they have no past record of governance and little credibility when it comes to policy. The same applies to newly transformed parties (e.g., splinters, mergers) yet to a lesser degree. The findings of Chapter Five show that voters are generally disinclined to hand over policy making to unknown or lesser known political formations. When faced with two equidistant parties in terms of policy, voters will generally prefer the party that has a long and familiar record over the newcomer. Given the higher risk and uncertainty associated with new formations, this decision can be interpreted as a lucid and reasoned one on the part of voters. When it comes to political representation and policy making, voters' tendency to minimise uncertainty implies a certain level of continuity and stability in electoral politics and the harbouring of governing expertise over electoral cycles. Hence the potential destabilising effects of party instability are minimised thanks to voters' demonstrated conservatism when it comes to voting for unknown party initiatives.

The final chapter also speaks well of voters' capacity to screen through important information and apply economic considerations to their vote choice *when such considerations are credible.* I have argued that economic retrospections

---

1. A case in point is the election of the radical-left party SYRIZA in the January 2015 election in Greece. Over the course of eight or so months into office, the politics of the core of the party were palpably driven towards the mainstream. Flanagan and Dalton (1984, p. 9) explain that new parties like SYRIZA tend to become 'socialised into the realities and limitations of effective political change and the need for compromise to achieve any progress.'

alone would not offer voters a good sense of governing capacity when parties themselves have transformed. Like several other scholars in political behaviour (Kedar 2009; Maravall 2006), my argument rests on the premise that voting is ultimately about who will govern in the future. Even voting on economic retrospections seeks to evaluate the future governing capacity of parties. When parties have transformed, economic retrospections alone cannot offer voters a good sense of their governing capacities after the election. The validity of economic evaluations is thus conditional on assessing how well past performance can predict governing competence after organisational changes. The results in Chapter Six give credence to this argument. The predicted odds of economic voting are half as likely when parties are unstable. These results show that voters do not reward (punish) for reward's (punishment's) sake. Rather, voters weigh economic retrospections against other important considerations (i.e., organisational change) to evaluate governing capacity. Using this strategy, voters are considerably more likely to elect competent policy makers into office than would be relying pure economic voting in contexts of party change.

We could argue further – to the voter's credit – that parties are not able to 'trick' voters through electoral manoeuvring. Consider that parties may resort to organisational changes for the purpose of redirecting public attention from a poor record of governance and onto a charismatic new leader or an alliance with a popular party. As Baekgaard and Jensen (2012, 135) write, parties may replace an unpopular leader, 'hoping that a new face will win the favour of the voters.' Incumbents may enter a strategic electoral alliance with another party which enjoys a favourable record of governance, or is otherwise popular, in order to increase their chances of electoral success. In another scenario, a faction of party members may abandon the organisation or a previously formed alliance and compete as an independent party in an attempt to distance itself from a poor record of governance or a public image of incompetence.

The empirical results in Chapter Six show that voters do not fall prey to such electoral manoeuvring. When voters evaluate performance poorly, party change can do little to cast incumbents in a positive light. In turn, even when voters evaluate the economy positively, they will not necessarily re-elect incumbents; voters are considerably less likely to do so when those incumbents have transformed. The latter result signals that voters weigh economic retrospections against the transformations incumbents have undergone. These results suggest that parties cannot easily sweep a poor record of governance under the rug or trick voters into re-electing them by initiating organisational changes. Even in highly complex elections with many new and transformed parties, voters remain prudent decision-makers.

A context-focused approach to comparative political behaviour

When I began working on this project, I was interested in the extent to which voters can make sound decisions in complex environments. I was influenced by the work of Lau and Redlawsk (2001, 2006) on correct voting as well as the large subfield on economic retrospective voting. Essentially, I wanted to know whether or not political representation and electoral accountability worked reasonably well when parties were in flux. I asked some of the following questions: Do voters elect similarly-minded policy makers to represent their interests in office? Do citizens sanction incumbents effectively for their performance in office? Do electoral representation and accountability hold up under unstable parties? My initial take fell under the approach advocated by Lau and Redlawsk (2006) in the following excerpt:

> This research proposes a new normative focus for the scientific study of voting behavio-r: We should care about not just which candidate received the most votes, but also how many citizens voted *correctly* – that is, in accordance with their own fully informed preferences.

However, once I had answered these questions – in the negative – I still could not answer *how* voters made decisions in such contexts. If voters did not rely on proximity or economic considerations, then how *did* they decide? Grappling with this latter question led me to revisit my initial approach to voter behaviour. At first, I was motivated by a normative concern with how voters ought to behave *across elections*. Since I was familiar with the quintessential theories of vote choice, I knew the standards to which voters should measure up. Much like Lau and Redlawsk, I was essentially holding up a bar to voters and classifying the outcome of their decisions in binary fashion, either as satisfactory and good for electoral democracy, or not.

Over time, however, I found this approach lacking. I began to question if there is just a single path to electoral representation and accountability suited across all electoral contexts. I also began to wonder why we should expect voters embedded in starkly different contexts to use the same rules to make electoral decisions. And perhaps I even developed some empathy with the voter embedded in a strained informational environment; for she faced a great deal more electoral uncertainty and likely experienced some anxiety and/or enthusiasm in facing new party formations. In the end I found the question of *how* such a voter made electoral decisions more interesting and theoretically enriching than the simpler, binary question of whether or not the outcome of her vote met my set of preconceived expectations.

The book is the product of this journey. Rather than asking whether or not voters conform to specific standards of reasoned decision-making, I have centred my research around the question of *how* voters make decisions in complex electoral spaces with specific characteristics. Granted, these questions are essentially two faces of the same coin. Answers to the latter invariably carry implications for the former; however, the former cannot necessarily provide answers to the latter.

What is more, each approach carries a set of implications about how we conceive of voters and the way we go about studying political behaviour. My initial approach conceived of voters as individual units that should all conform to a set of standards on political decision-making. Using this approach, I examined electoral behaviour across contexts with a set of preconceived notions of how decision-making should unfold. The approach that I have favoured throughout the book has instead conceived of voters as individuals who, under different circumstances and in different contexts, face more or less difficult decisions. The latter approach allowed me to go about the study of their behaviour by first focusing on the specific context in which such voters found themselves and then formulating expectations about voter behaviour based on the specific hurdles voters faced in each context.

Using each of the two approaches consecutively, I came to rather different – and contradictory – conclusions about voters. In measuring voter decisions against a set of standards on political knowledge and proximity and economic voting, I came to the conclusion that voters in elections with high party instability are rather unknowledgeable about party positions and fall short of being competent electoral decision-makers. In retrospect, this approach seems all too quick to label voters as misinformed and incompetent without giving due credit to the difficult circumstances (i.e., high informational costs) they faced in erratic elections. The approach I ultimately adopted – from understanding context to deriving expectations about decision-making mechanisms to understanding the normative implications of those decisions – allowed me to appreciate the versatility of voters facing cognitively taxing electoral contexts. As I argued at the beginning of this chapter, the process of their decision-making is efficient in making full use of scarce informational resources. What is more, the outcomes of their decisions did not necessarily contradict principles of electoral representation, suggesting that alternative routes to electoral democracy are at work.

The findings in Chapter Six illustrate the advantages to employing a context-focused approach. Had we not considered the context of party instability, we would have come to the misguided conclusion that voters cannot make sense of the electoral environment and that parties are able to distract voters from economic considerations (given the lower rates of economic voting in erratic elections) onto alternative considerations (e.g., party leaders' charisma). A good understanding of party instability and its implications for the economic vote allows us instead to interpret these findings in a starkly different light. In the case of high party change, lower rates of economic voting spell good news for electoral accountability and political representation. They indicate that voters can ingenuously juxtapose two pieces of potentially contradictory information – one on the state of the economy and another one on the history of party change. It is only when parties are organisationally continuous that voters can rely on the latter piece of information to determine governing capacity. The result must be one of the first studies not to alarm its readers on low levels of economic voting but to celebrate voters' prudence in considering additional – and potentially contradictory – information. The approach parts ways with the one adopted initially and one that is based on the well-entrenched belief that economic voting is universal and should be upheld across elections.

I do not wish to deny the advantages of the Lau and Redlawsk approach which seeks to identify a set of decision-making rules universally upheld across contexts. Their approach is well suited to experimental settings and has the advantage of limited endogeneity between cause and effect. A context-specific approach, though certainly not as clean in terms of internal validity, nonetheless examines politics in more dynamic and realistic terms. By studying the processes of electoral decision-making – from context to decision-making mechanisms to normative implications – we can understand how and when voters' decision-making processes conform to extant theories and when and why they do not. The approach I advocate does not take for granted that voters will behave uniformly when their informational environments differ systematically. It places a great deal of import on the characteristics of the electoral context. It considers carefully their implications for the costs of information and the decision-making tools voters have more readily at their disposal. It derives context-specific expectations about voter behaviour that test the limits of extant theories in political behaviour. Had we not examined the role of party instability, we may well have come to the misguided conclusion that voters across many elections in Europe (e.g., those facing party instability) make poor electoral decisions that do not meet our prior expectations of sound electoral choice. The present account instead documents *how* voters decide and celebrates their ingenuity in adopting coping mechanisms for electoral complexity.

The contribution of parties to political behaviour

This book is not the first to investigate the link between parties and voters; yet it may well be the first to link specific party behaviour to voters' decision-making. Earlier research has developed at the level of party systems rather than the individual party. For example, previous literature has studied the effects of multi-party systems, the competitiveness of the electoral race and the polarisation of party positions for the ability of voters to acquire and apply information on political ideology to their vote choice (Basinger and Lavine 2005; Berggren 2001; Ensley 2007; Gordon and Segura 1997; Lachat 2008). Each of the explanatory factors – multi-party systems, electoral competitiveness and party polarisation – are studied at the level of party systems. The present book has closely examined the behaviour of individual parties instead and has linked changes in each party to voters' political behaviour, including their levels of political knowledge and the vote. As such, it stands apart from earlier research that had steadily remained at the level of party systems.

The advantage of this book's take on the party-voter nexus is that it allows for party agency. In other words, parties are not passive recipients of voter evaluations but can influence the processes of voter information acquisition and decision-making. Because information on individual parties' manoeuvring the electoral landscape is cumbersome to collect, the rich and intricate world of party organisations had thus far not been integrated into the study of comparative political behaviour.[2] The detailed data collected on party organisations across 148 European elections enabled the study to move away from static accounts of

---

2. It is worth noting that earlier research has examined some aspects of party behaviour, but it has done so on a single case or a limited number of cases (e.g., Dix 1992; Kreuzer and Pettai 2003; Shabad and Slomczynski 2004).

party-voter interaction and to endow parties with the agency to shape the political behaviour of voters. In and of itself, this approach is gratifying as it conceives of elections in fairly realistic terms – as dynamic, give-and-take interactions between voters and parties.

What is more, the evidence presented in this book leaves little doubt that the actions of political parties influence the ways in which voters make decisions. Voter behaviour, as formulated in extant theories of electoral decision-making, is conditional on the effective fulfilment of parties' informational functions – namely, to organise and communicate electoral alternatives to voters. When parties communicate a fixed and stable set of electoral alternatives, they ease the gathering of political information and the usage of a set of judgmental shortcuts by voters. Abrupt organisational changes in turn are associated with lower levels of political knowledge and the usage of a different set of informational heuristics. New and transformed parties may well offer consistent and ideologically coherent programs (cf. Rohrschneider and Whitefield 2012), but they are not as effective in communicating those alternatives to voters as are stable and well-known parties. The messages of new or newly transformed parties are more difficult to attribute correctly as those parties are less familiar to the voter. Party instability places greater cognitive demands on voters, such that voters have difficulty taking party cues, as evidenced by their lower levels of knowledge about party positions in erratic elections. The politically sophisticated voters, who are generally more likely to know and use information on party ideology in their electoral calculus, are no more likely to choose ideologically than are the less sophisticated when party instability is just moderately high. We can thus discern that political parties have an important facilitating function in electoral decision-making.

The evidence from this book further shows that the quintessential theories of political behaviour – proximity voting, economic voting – are conditional on party behaviour. Such theories were formulated based on the experiences of 'clean' electoral contexts where electoral alternatives were assumed to be fixed; and where parties were assumed to communicate their positions clearly and effectively, and to do so equally well. These are strong assumptions that are met in few elections. The reality of electoral landscapes is that they are rather messy and inconstant over electoral cycles. Parties are continuously in flux, regenerating and transforming themselves. Some parties will invariably have more credibility than others, and their message will be louder and clearer. Parties' organisational changes alone provide considerable variation in and challenge the strong assumptions of extant theories. The manoeuvring of party organisations renders these theories relative rather than universal and invites us to examine in greater detail the characteristics of the informational environments in which voters find themselves and the role of political parties therein.

Directions for future research

This book represents an initial attempt to understand how political parties shape electoral information environments, facilitate the use of political ideology as a heuristic and influence the ways in which voters make decisions. Far from having a final say on these subjects, the findings of the book leave many unanswered questions for future research to take up. In conclusion, I offer some thoughts on three of these questions that seem most pressing and of greatest potential to enrich our knowledge of representative democracy.

The first path to research evokes a comparative dimension to future research in political psychology. Indeed, the findings of this book give due credit to Paul Sniderman's call to consider not only voter characteristics in the use of heuristics but also the structure of electoral spaces in facilitating their usage. No doubt that the characteristics of citizens continue to hold much of the explanatory power. This contribution has made clear that, in addition, differences between electoral contexts influence voters' information acquisition and decision-making rules. Indeed, voters across electoral contexts adapt to varying levels of complexity by relying on a unique set of decision-making rules to elect their political representatives. These results should motivate further research on the political and institutional conditionalities of heuristics' use (cf. Carmines and D'Amico 2015). Any attempt to understand how the structure of electoral spaces influences the use of heuristics should employ a comparative dimension. Extant research in political psychology has been narrowly informed by the experiences of mature democracies, and primarily that of the United States. As it stands, the field would benefit from comparative research which could inform the ways in which variation in the information environment conditions political behaviour.

A second promising path to understanding the linkages between parties and voters centres on political socialisation. The data amassed in this book alone spans several decades, each with a unique set of political events. One cannot help but wonder if the effects of party instability on voters in the new democracies in Central and Eastern Europe in the early 1990s were the same as equivalent levels of party instability in, say, the 2000s. Along the same lines, one also wonders if a voter coming of age in the recent turbulent elections in Greece may carry with her a set of unique decision-making mechanisms along her life cycle as a voter that may set her apart from a voter who experienced the same type of instability towards the end of her life cycle. We know that the influence of the political environment is most noticeable among new voters who experienced changes in their environments in the formative years of their lives (Franklin 2004; Hooghe 2004; Jennings 1987) and that this is particularly pronounced in new political regimes (Mishler and Rose 2007). Indeed the party instability experienced in the new European democracies in the 1990s is such a defining feature of the electoral landscape (Bielasiak 2002), that, when it comes to electoral politics, it may well be characterised as a generation-defining event with potential consequences for the political socialisation of an entire cohort of voters. Because primary socialisation experiences produce persistent effects on voter behaviour (Hooghe 2004; Langton 1984), the effects of party instability from the early years of democratisation likely continue to matter for voter behaviour and public policy – despite the fact that instability has long subsided. More broadly, a fruitful venue for future research is to understand how differences in information environments shape early experiences of political socialisation and their long-run effects on political predispositions and decision-making.

The third and final venue for future research I wish to mention here is the role of the mass media. Unfortunately this important element in the chain of electoral information was out of the scope of this book. It is important to emphasise that the media hold the key to understanding political communication and voters' information environments and should take centre stage in future research. As we saw in Chapter Four, voters in several turbulent elections in the new European democracies enjoyed relatively high levels of political knowledge. A close examination of these particular cases revealed the positive role of the media. When the mass media offer ample coverage of the electoral campaign, they are in a unique position to offset the informational costs of high party turnover. A number of interesting questions remain to be answered in this respect. How do the media portray changing parties – as risky electoral alternatives to be avoided or as exciting newcomers to be taken seriously? Do the media devote more air time to parties that undergo organisational changes than to those that do not? When it comes to new and newly transformed parties, do the media stress the programmatic aspects of the campaign or more sensational aspects (e.g., political personalities, scandals)? Relatedly, do the media provide voters with reliable policy information in complex electoral environments to the same extent that it does in elections with stable parties? Because the voter relies on the mass media for electoral information, the answers to these questions are crucial to understanding political decision-making, citizen-elite linkages and electoral representation.

Appendix: Party Instability Data

Inclusion thresholds

I apply different criteria for mergers and joint lists at the party and election levels of analysis. Recording the sheer number of parties involved in mergers and joint lists at the election level would give undue weight to these categories, as, by definition, two or more parties are involved in these types of party change (merger, joint list entry and joint list exit). As a consequence, mergers and joint lists changes would, by design, insert at least twice the weight of new party formations in the overall index. Empirically, this can be easily observed in Figure 3.1 where the average number of parties participating in mergers, joint list entry and joint list exit is several times higher than the average number of new, disbanded or splinter parties in a given election. To correct for this, I record the number of new or modified mergers and joint lists, regardless of the number of parties comprising each. Accordingly, I implement the inclusion threshold at the level of mergers or joint lists rather than at the level of parties.

Party-level data

New party: The 5 per cent threshold is applied at *t*.
Disbanded party: The 5 per cent threshold is applied at *t-1*.
Splinter: The 5 per cent threshold is applied at *t*.
Merger: To exclude marginal parties from the index, at least two of the merged parties must have received 5 per cent of the vote or more at *t-1* and the merger must receive over 5 per cent at *t*.
Joint lists (two indicators: entry, exit): To exclude marginal parties from the index, the 5 per cent threshold is applied as follows: for entry, at least two of the parties must have received 5 per cent of the vote or more at *t-1* and the joint list must receive over 5 per cent at *t*; for exit, the joint list must have received 5 per cent of the vote or more at *t-1*, and each of the parties must receive over 5 per cent at *t*.

Election-level data (EIP index)

New party: The 5 per cent threshold is applied at *t*.
Disbanded party: The 5 per cent threshold is applied at *t-1*.
Splinter: The 5 per cent threshold is applied at *t*.

Merger: A merger is included in the index if it passed the 5 per cent threshold at *t*. Joint list (entry, exit): A new joint list forms part of the index when (a) a new joint list formed or a party entered an existing joint list and (b) the joint list passed the 5 per cent threshold at *t*. A disbanded joint list is included when (a) a joint list disbanded between elections *t* and *t-1* or a member of the joint list at *t-1* abandoned it by *t* and (b) the joint list received 5 per cent of the vote or more at *t-1*.

Table A.1: List of parliamentary elections

Country	First election	Last election	Number of elections
Austria	November 23, 1986	September 28, 2008	7
Belgium	December 13, 1987	June 13, 2010	6
Bulgaria	June 10, 1990	July 5, 2009	6
Czech Republic	May 31, 1996	May 28, 2010	4
Denmark	September 8, 1987	November 13, 2007	7
Estonia	September 20, 1992	March 6, 2011	5
Finland	March 16, 1987	April 17, 2011	6
France	June 5, 1988	June 10, 2007	4
Germany	January 25, 1987	September 27, 2009	6
Greece	June 18, 1989	October 4, 2009	8
Hungary	March 25, 1990	April 11, 2010	5
Iceland	April 25, 1987	April 25, 2009	6
Ireland	February 17, 1987	February 25, 2011	6
Italy	March 28, 1994	April 13, 2008	4
Latvia	June 5, 1993	October 2, 2010	5
Lithuania	November 15, 1992	October 12, 2008	4
Netherlands	September 6, 1989	June 9, 2010	6
Norway	September 11, 1989	September 14, 2009	5
Poland	October 27, 1991	October 21, 2007	5
Portugal	July 19, 1987	September 27, 2009	6
Romania	May 20, 1990	November 30, 2008	5
Slovakia	June 9, 1990	June 12, 2010	5
Slovenia	April 8, 1990	September 21, 2008	5
Spain	October 29, 1989	March 9, 2008	5
Sweden	September 18, 1988	September 19, 2010	6
Switzerland	October 18, 1987	October 21, 2007	5
United Kingdom	June 11, 1987	May 6, 2010	5

Table A.2: Summary statistics of EIP, by country

Country	Mean	Min	Max	SD
Austria	0.14	0	1	0.38
Belgium	2	0	4	1.41
Bulgaria	7.3	3	10	2.7
Czech Republic	1.5	1	2	0.58
Denmark	0.14	0	1	0.38
Estonia	7	0	17	6.5
Finland	0.2	0	1	0.4
France	0.5	0	2	1
Germany	1	0	2	0.9
Greece	0.25	0	1	0.5
Hungary	1.6	0	5	1.9
Iceland	1.4	0	2	0.8
Ireland	0.2	0	1	0.4
Italy	4.75	4	6	1
Latvia	5.8	4	8	2
Lithuania	5.75	2	10	3.3
Netherlands	0.33	0	1	0.52
Norway	0	0	0	0
Poland	5.2	2	10	3.1
Portugal	0	0	0	0
Romania	4.2	3	6	1.3
Slovakia	3.6	1	7	2.4
Slovenia	2.8	1	4	1.3
Spain	0	0	0	0
Sweden	0.2	0	1	0.4
Switzerland	0	0	0	0
United Kingdom	0.4	0	2	0.9

Table A.3: Summary statistics of variables

Variable	Mean	SD	Range	N
Individual-per-party level				
Ideological distance from party	2.60	1.93	0,10	451484
Political knowledge of party	8.34	1.51	0,10	390387

Table A.3 (*continued*)

Variable	Mean	SD	Range	N
Individual level				
Age	47.4	16.9	17,100	79125
Male	.50	.5	0,1	79125
University degree	.16	.37	0,1	79125
Party level				
Party age	44.8	41.7	0,171	310
New party	.02	.15	0,1	310
Merged party	.04	.19	0,1	310
Splinter party	.04	.19	0,1	310
Entered joint list	.04	.19	0,1	310
Exited joint list	.02	.14	0,1	310
Party strength	15.25	11.84	.87,45	310
Election level				
EIP	1.4	2.2	0,10	55
EIP (log)	1.51	0.27	1,2.3	55
MDM	18.4	37.5	1,150	55
PR system	.84	.37	0,1	55
Majoritarian system	.05	.23	0,1	55
Bicameral legislature	.51	.5	0,1	55
Months since previous election	46.6	8.7	23.8,61.6	55
Compulsory voting	0.4	.19	0,1	55
Seat-vote disparity	4.1	3.6	.1, 15.78	55

Table A.4: EIP scores by country (CSES elections)

Country	N	Mean	Std. Dev.	Min.	Max.
Austria	1	0	.	.	.
Bulgaria	1	10	.	.	.
Czech Republic	3	1.67	.06	1	2
Denmark	3	.3	.6	0	1
Estonia	1	0	.	.	.
Finland	3	0	0	0	0
France	1	2	.	.	.
Germany	4	.5	.6	0	1
Greece	1	0	.	.	.

Table A.4 (*continued*)

Country	N	Mean	Std. Dev.	Min.	Max.
Hungary	2	1	0	1	1
Iceland	3	1.7	.6	1	2
Ireland	2	.5	.7	0	1
Italy	1	4	.	.	.
Latvia	1	5	.	.	.
Netherlands	4	.5	.6	0	1
Norway	3	0	0	0	0
Poland	4	5.3	3.6	2	10
Portugal	3	0	0	0	0
Romania	2	4	1.4	3	5
Slovakia	1	2	.	.	.
Slovenia	3	2.7	1.5	1	4
Spain	3	0	0	0	0
Sweden	3	0	0	0	0
Switzerland	3	0	0	0	0
United Kingdom	2	0	0	0	0

Note: The table lists the number of election studies per country, mean EIP score, standard deviation and range. When only one election study was available per country, its EIP score is listed in the Mean column. The elections included in the study are Austria, 2008; Bulgaria 2001; Czech Republic 2002, 2006, 2010; Denmark, 1998, 2001, 2007; Estonia 2011; Finland, 2003, 2007, 2011; France, 2007; Germany, 1998, 2002, 2005, 2009; Hungary 1998, 2002; Iceland 2003, 2007, 2009; Ireland, 2002, 2007; Italy, 2006; Latvia 2010; Netherlands, 1998, 2002, 2006, 2010; Norway, 2001, 2005, 2009; Poland 1997, 2001, 2005, 2007; Portugal, 2002, 2005, 2009; Romania 1996, 2004; Slovakia 2010; Slovenia 1996, 2004, 2008; Spain, 1996, 2004, 2008; Sweden, 1998, 2002, 2006; Switzerland, 1999, 2003, 2007; Great Britain, 1997, 2005.

Coding of party positions in Estonia-2011

There are inconsistencies in how CSES *experts* coded parties' left-right positions (0-left; 10-right; variables C5017_A to C5017_F in Module 3). As can be seen from the table below, CSES experts were hugely off in placing parties, as compared to both voters and an independent expert survey (Vowles, Hellwig and Coffey, 2009 who use the same scale). Take party C, the conservative Union Pro Patria and Res Publica. CSES voters and Vowles *et al.* both place this party on the right of the left-right scale whereas CSES experts rank the party on the extreme left. These coding mistakes explain why initially voters in Estonia-2011 seem to perform comparatively poorly in terms of political knowledge and why this election stood out as an outlier in terms of the dependent variable. To correct this, I have used the Vowles *et al.* expert placements of parties (rounded to the nearest digit) and have rerun all analyses. After the correction, Estonia has about average rates of political knowledge, in line with what we would expect from the low levels of party instability in that election.

Table A.5: Party positions in Estonia-2011

Party	Average voter placement (CSES)	CSES expert	Vowles *et al.* expert survey (2009)
A	7.7	4	8
B	3.2	7	4
C	7	1	7.7
D	4.7	9	4.3
E	4.1	2	4.7
F	4.9	3	5

Appendix to Chapter Four

Outliers: Italy, Bulgaria and Poland

First, an anyalysis of the residuals from the null model of political knowledge revealed several potential outliers. I performed a Cook's Distances test for the election-level observations in order to assess the influence and leverage of each observation on the model. Bulgaria-2001 has both high leverage and influence while Poland-2001 has high leverage but low influence and Italy-2006 has high influence but low leverage. Removing either Bulgaria-2001 or Italy-2006 substantially changes coefficient estimates; while Poland has an extreme value on the predictor variable, its removal does not substantially change the estimates of the regression. I include binary variables for Bulgaria-2001, Italy-2006 and Poland-2001 in all models.

Table A.6: Knowledge of party positions: controlling for media freedom

	(1)	(2)	(3)
Party Instability			
New party	−0.409***	−0.409***	0.106***
	0.0170	0.0170	0.0284
Merged	0.204***	0.204***	0.398***
	0.0141	0.0141	0.0197
JL Entry	0.203***	0.203***	0.334***
	0.0197	0.0197	0.0240
Splinter	−0.130***	−0.130***	−0.066**
	0.0156	0.0156	0.0238
JL Exit	−0.643***	−0.643***	−0.534***
	0.0271	0.0271	0.0285
EIP	−0.053		−0.094
	0.0350		0.0494
Education			
University education	0.292***	0.289***	0.292***
	0.0085	0.0086	0.0085
EIP, centr.		−0.051	
		0.0350	
EIP * University education		−0.013**	
		0.0044	
Region			
Western Europe			0.036
			0.1374
New party * W. Europe			−0.833***
			0.0355
Merged * W. Europe			−0.425***
			0.0281
JL Entry * W. Europe			−0.132**
			0.0476
Splinter * W. Europe			−0.055
			0.0341
EIP * W. Europe			0.151
			0.0880
Control Variables			
Age	0.004***	0.004***	0.004***

Table A.6 (*continued*)

	(1)	(2)	(3)
	0.0011	0.0011	0.0011
Age * Age	−0.000***	−0.000***	−0.000***
	0.0000	0.0000	0.0000
Male	0.118***	0.000	0.118***
	0.0063	.	0.0063
Distance from party	−0.071***	−0.071***	−0.070***
	0.0012	0.0012	0.0012
ENEP, log	−0.238	−0.239	−0.174
	0.2044	0.2043	0.2015
MDM	0.001	0.001	0.001
	0.0010	0.0010	0.0009
Proportional	0.182	0.183	0.240*
	0.1154	0.1153	0.1151
Majoritarian	0.144	0.146	0.093
	0.1920	0.1919	0.2035
Bicameral legislature	−0.021	−0.020	−0.001
	0.0824	0.0823	0.0804
Months since last election	0.002	0.002	0.002
	0.0045	0.0045	0.0044
Compulsory voting	0.000	0.000	0.000
	.	.	.
Seat-vote disparity	−0.003	−0.003	0.003
	0.0190	0.0190	0.0188
Media freedom	−0.019**	−0.019**	−0.016*
	0.0070	0.0070	0.0073
Italy - 2006	−0.807**	−0.810**	−1.316***
	0.2737	0.2736	0.3726
Bulgaria - 2001	0.990*	0.985*	1.091*
	0.3972	0.3970	0.4650
Poland - 2001	0.066	0.063	0.357
	0.3892	0.3890	0.4503
Constant	8.826***	8.759***	8.580***
	0.3483	0.3703	0.3835
Variance Components			
Intercept (respondent)	0.0582	0.0581	0.3716

Table A.6 (*continued*)

	(1)	(2)	(3)
	0.0115	0.0115	0.0039
Intercept (election)	0.3707	0.3707	0.0543
	0.0039	0.0039	0.0107
N	379,814	379,814	379,814

Note: Coefficients and standard errors from a three-level model of political knowledge are reported. The sample contains 379,814 respondent-party pairs from 72, 207 respondents in 53 elections. Data on media freedom come from the Freedom House, where 0 is most free and 100 is least free. Coefficient estimates are maximum likelihood unstandardised coefficients. Analyses were performed in Stata 12 with the .xtmixed command. $*p < 0.05$, $**p < 0.01$, $***p < 0.001$

Appendix to Chapter Six

Table A.7: Mixed-effects logistic model of vote for Prime Minister's party

	All elections: EIP (1)	All elections: EIP and Clarity (2)	Low clarity elections (3)	High clarity elections (4)	All elections: Full spec. (5)
Age	0.007***	0.007***	0.006***	0.008***	0.007***
	0.0007	0.0007	0.0009	0.0013	0.0007
Male	–0.047	–0.048	–0.069*	–0.004	–0.048
	0.0245	0.0246	0.0297	0.0439	0.0246
University education	–0.180***	–0.183***	–0.180***	–0.190***	–0.185***
	0.0318	0.0320	0.0385	0.0571	0.0321
Ideological distance	–0.045***	–0.044***	–0.031***	–0.076***	–0.045***
	0.0016	0.0016	0.0019	0.0033	0.0016
Electoral instability (EIP)	–0.186*	–0.200*	–0.219*	–0.082	–0.122
	0.0819	0.0855	0.1048	0.1792	0.1656
Performance evaluation					
Very poor	(base)	(base)	(base)	(base)	(base)
Poor	0.647***	0.676***	0.289***	0.962***	0.659***
	0.0504	0.0522	0.0657	0.0879	0.0531
Good	1.892***	1.968***	1.399***	2.455***	1.885***
	0.0524	0.0543	0.0670	0.0926	0.0554
Very good	2.615***	2.828***	2.006***	3.797***	2.883***
	0.0835	0.0905	0.0987	0.2084	0.1133
Performance x EIP					
Very poor x EIP	(base)	(base)	(base)	(base)	(base)
Poor x EIP	0.007	0.091***	0.049*	0.003	0.170***
	0.0178	0.0199	0.0189	0.0851	0.0417
Good x EIP	–0.015	0.148***	0.047	–0.019	0.373***
	0.0231	0.0251	0.0247	0.0890	0.0475
Very good x EIP	–0.095*	0.063	–0.011	–0.469**	0.127
	0.0417	0.0428	0.0427	0.1649	0.0863

Table A.7 (*continued*)

	All elections: EIP (1)	All elections: EIP and Clarity (2)	Low clarity elections (3)	High clarity elections (4)	All elections: Full spec. (5)
Performance x Clarity					
Very poor x Clarity		−0.051			−0.061
		0.0412			0.0456
Poor x Clarity		0.072			0.046
		0.0403			0.0446
Good x Clarity		0.151***			0.097*
		0.0403			0.0448
Very good x Clarity		0.200***			0.194***
		0.0427			0.0517
Performance x EIP x Clarity					
Very poor x EIP x Clarity					0.012
					0.0247
Poor x EIP x Clarity					0.028
					0.0243
Good x EIP x Clarity					0.064**
					0.0247
Very good x EIP x Clarity					0.023
					0.0291
Constant	−1.805***	−1.832***	−1.633***	−1.888***	−1.873***
	0.2173	0.2046	0.3356	0.1904	0.2088
Variance components					
Intercept	1.357***	1.179***	1.995***	0.255***	1.147***
	0.324	0.281	0.603	0.096	0.272
Ni / Nj	42,173/ 42	42,173/42	29,357/ 27	12,816/ 15	42,173/ 42

Note: Table 1 reports coefficient estimates from a mixed-effects logistic regression. The dependent variable is vote for the prime minister's party. Models 3 and 4 partition the sample into elections with low (below 0) and high clarity of responsibility (above 0). $*p < 0.05$, $**p < 0.01$, $***p < 0.001$

Table A.8: Mixed-effects logistic regression for incumbent vote by instability in incumbent parties

	All elections: EIP (1)	All elections: EIP and Clarity (2)	Low clarity elections (3)	High clarity elections (4)	All elections: Full spec. (5)
Age	0.006***	0.007***	0.004***	0.012***	0.007***
	0.0007	0.0007	0.0008	0.0013	0.0007
Male	−0.032	−0.033	−0.062*	0.038	−0.033
	0.0225	0.0226	0.0265	0.0429	0.0226
University education	−0.005	−0.003	0.051	−0.137*	−0.005
	0.0287	0.0289	0.0338	0.0548	0.0289
Ideological distance	−0.048***	−0.048***	−0.036***	−0.080***	−0.048***
	0.0014	0.0014	0.0016	0.0031	0.0014
Electoral instability in incumbent parties (EIP-I)	−0.204	−0.477***	−0.335*	0.724	−0.026
	0.1253	0.1408	0.1401	0.4812	0.3173
Performance evaluation					
Very poor	(base)	(base)	(base)	(base)	(base)
Poor	0.581***	0.688***	0.285***	0.990***	0.750***
	0.0412	0.0437	0.0520	0.0727	0.0466
Good	1.823***	2.053***	1.392***	2.535***	2.110***
	0.0434	0.0467	0.0539	0.0784	0.0493
Very good	2.643***	3.162***	2.073***	3.922***	3.265***
	0.0749	0.0925	0.0867	0.1743	0.0989
Performance x EIP-I					
Very poor x EIP	(base)	(base)	(base)	(base)	(base)
Poor x EIP	−0.045	0.182***	0.072	−0.445**	−0.118
	0.0383	0.0441	0.0410	0.1577	0.0829
Good x EIP	−0.084	0.438***	0.079	−0.336	0.149
	0.0479	0.0534	0.0502	0.1936	0.1081
Very good x EIP	−0.207*	0.488***	0.026	−1.102**	−0.094
	0.0961	0.1027	0.0988	0.3765	0.2089
Performance x Clarity					
Very poor x Clarity		−0.132***			−0.162***

Table A.8 (*continued*)

	All elections: EIP (1)	All elections: EIP and Clarity (2)	Low clarity elections (3)	High clarity elections (4)	All elections: Full spec. (5)
		0.0293			0.0307
Poor x Clarity		−0.025			−0.027
		0.0286			0.0296
Good x Clarity		0.073*			0.068*
		0.0287			0.0297
Very good x Clarity		0.178***			0.184***
		0.0335			0.0351
Performance x EIP-I x Clarity					
Very poor x EIP x Clarity					0.071
					0.0416
Poor x EIP x Clarity					0.021
					0.0409
Good x EIP x Clarity					0.024
					0.0415
Very good x EIP x Clarity					−0.023
					0.0488
Constant	−1.095***	−1.250***	−0.769***	−1.637***	−1.323***
	0.1417	0.1432	0.1911	0.1948	0.1453
Variance components					
Intercept	0.596***	0.596***	0.670***	0.369***	0.582***
	0.132	0.132	0.184	0.138	0.129
Ni / Nj	42,173/ 42	42,173/42	29,357/ 27	12,816/ 15	42,173/ 42

Table A.9: Mixed-effects logistic regression for incumbent vote by instability in opposition parties

	All elections: EIP (1)	All elections: EIP and Clarity (2)	Low clarity elections (3)	High clarity elections (4)	All elections: Full spec. (5)
Age	0.006***	0.007***	0.004***	0.012***	0.007***
	0.0007	0.0007	0.0008	0.0013	0.0007
Male	−0.032	−0.034	−0.062*	0.040	−0.034
	0.0225	0.0226	0.0266	0.0429	0.0226
University education	−0.005	−0.002	0.052	−0.134*	−0.004
	0.0287	0.0289	0.0339	0.0548	0.0290
Ideological distance	−0.048***	−0.048***	−0.036***	−0.081***	−0.048***
	0.0014	0.0014	0.0016	0.0031	0.0014
Electoral instability in opposition parties (EIP-O)	−0.088	−0.236*	−0.154	0.050	−0.311
	0.0888	0.0961	0.1032	0.2411	0.1615
Performance evaluation					
Very poor	(base)	(base)	(base)	(base)	(base)
Poor	0.629***	0.692***	0.340***	0.941***	0.689***
	0.0446	0.0463	0.0578	0.0765	0.0470
Good	1.985***	2.107***	1.573***	2.560***	2.021***
	0.0484	0.0502	0.0614	0.0847	0.0508
Very good	2.915***	3.299***	2.389***	4.060***	3.199***
	0.0860	0.0978	0.0984	0.2229	0.1184
Performance x EIP-O					
Very poor x EIP	(base)	(base)	(base)	(base)	(base)
Poor x EIP	−0.051*	0.080**	0.015	−0.095	0.132**
	0.0233	0.0265	0.0254	0.0885	0.0480
Good x EIP	−0.220***	0.036	−0.139***	−0.196*	0.305***
	0.0310	0.0333	0.0345	0.0926	0.0538
Very good x EIP	−0.381***	−0.097	−0.310***	−0.475*	0.143
	0.0614	0.0597	0.0670	0.1871	0.1057
Performance x Clarity					
Very poor x Clarity		−0.114***			−0.093**

Table A.9 (*continued*)

	All elections: EIP (1)	All elections: EIP and Clarity (2)	Low clarity elections (3)	High clarity elections (4)	All elections: Full spec. (5)
		0.0289			0.0357
Poor x Clarity		−0.014			−0.010
		0.0283			0.0345
Good x Clarity		0.060*			0.017
		0.0283			0.0347
Very good x Clarity		0.149***			0.108*
		0.0324			0.0446
Performance x EIP-O x Clarity					
Very poor x EIP x Clarity					−0.016
					0.0279
Poor x EIP x Clarity					−0.004
					0.0272
Good x EIP x Clarity					0.054*
					0.0274
Very good x EIP x Clarity					0.043
					0.0333
Constant	−1.142***	−1.227***	−0.839***	−1.543***	−1.214***
	0.1536	0.1525	0.2106	0.2113	0.1579
Variance components					
Intercept	0.628***	0.610***	0.724***	0.395***	0.637***
	0.139	0.135	0.199	0.147	0.141
Ni / Nj	42,173/ 42	42,173/42	29,357/ 27	12,816/ 15	42,173/42

Appendix: Party Names

Name in English	Original name	Abbrev.
Greece		
Panhellenic Socialist Movement	Πανελλήνιο Σοσιαλιστικό Κίνημα	PASOK
	Panellénio Sosialistikó Kínēma	
New Democracy	Νέα Δημοκρατία	ND
	Néa Dēmokratía	
Pact for a New Greece	Συμφωνία για τη Νέα Ελλάδα	
	Symphōnía gia tē Néa Elláda	
Union for the Homeland and the People	Ένωση για την Πατρίδα και τον Λαό	
	Énōsē gia tēn Patrída kai ton Laó	
Plan B	Σχέδιο B	
	Schédio B	
Reformers for Democracy and Development	Μεταρρυθμιστές για τη Δημοκρατία και την Ανάπτυξη	
	Metarrythmistés gia tē Dēmokratía kai tēn Anáptyxē	
The River	Το Ποτάμι	
	To Potámi	
Belgium		
People's Union	Volksunie	VU
Spirit	Spirit	
New Flemish Alliance	Nieuw-Vlaamse Alliantie	N-VA
People's Union-ID21	Volksunie -ID21	VU-ID21
Flemish Socialist Party	Socialistische Partij Anders	sp.a
Liberal Reformation Party	Parti Réformateur Libéral	PRL
Francophone Democratic Front	Démocrate Fédéraliste Indépendant	DéFI
Reformist Movement	Mouvement Réformateur	MR
Radical Innovators and Social Warriors for a Fairer Society	Radicale Omvormers en Sociale Strijders voor een Eerlijker Maatschappij	ROSSEM
Bulgaria		
Democrats for Strong Bulgaria	Демократи за силна България	DSB
	Demokrati za silna Bălgarija	
United Democratic Forces	Съюз на демократичните сили	SDS
	Săjuz na demokratičnite sili	
National Movement Simeon II	Национално движение Симеон II	NDSV
	Nacionalno dviženie Simeon II	

Name in English	Original name	Abbrev.
Netherlands		
General Elderly Alliance	Algemeen Ouderen Verbond	AOV
Slovenia		
Slovenia is Ours	Slovenija je naša	
Denmark		
Centre of Democrats	Centrum-Demokraterne	CD
Italy		
Liberal Party of Italy	Partito Liberale Italiano	PLI
L'Ulivo	The Olive Tree	
Democrats of the Left	Democratici di Sinistra	DS
Democracy is Freedom – The Daisy	Democrazia è Libertà – La Margherita	DL
Movement of European Republicans	Movimento Repubblicani Europei	MRE
North League	Lega Nord	LN
Movement for the Autonomies	Movimento per le Autonomie	MpA
Democratic Union of Centre	Unione di Centro	UdC
Union of Christian Democrats and Democrats of Centre	Unione dei Democratici Cristiani e di Centro	UDCe
Forward Italy	Forza Italia	FI
The People of Freedom	Il Popolo della Liberta	PdL
The Right–Tricolour Flame	La Destra – Fiamma Tricolore	
Partito Democratico	Democratic Party	PD
The Left – The Rainbow	La Sinistra - l'Arcobaleno	SA
Communist Refoundation Party	Partito della Rifondazione Comunista	PRC
National Alliance	Alleanza Nazionale	AN
Christian Democrats – the New Italian Socialist Party	Democrazia Cristiana per le Autonomie (DCA) - Nuovo Partito Socialista Italiano (Nuovo PSI)	DC-Nuovo PSI
Czech Republic		
Freedom Union	Unie Svobody	US
Civic Democratic Party	Občanská demokratická strana	ODS
Poland		
Polish Peasants' Party	Polskie Stronnictwo Ludowe	PSL
League of Polish Families	Liga Polskich Rodzin	LPR
Movement for Reconstruction of Poland	Ruch Odbudowy Polski	ROP
Civic Platform	Platforma Obywatelska	PO

Name in English	Original name	Abbrev.
Freedom Union	Unia Wolności	UW
Samoobrana Rzeczpospolitej Polskiej	Self-Defence of the Republic of Poland	SRP
Democratic Left Alliance	Sojusz Lewicy Demokratycznej	SLD
Union of Labor	Unia Pracy	UP
Right of the Republic	Prawica Rzeczypospolitej	
Self-Defence of the Republic of Poland – National Party of Retirees and Pensioners	Samoobrona Rzeczpospolitej Polskiej-Krajowa Partia Emerytów i Rencistów	SRP-KPEiR
Law and Justice	Prawo i Sprawiedliwość	PiS
Iceland		
Social Democratic Alliance	Samfylkingin-Jafnaðarmannaflokkur Íslands	Samfylkingin
Ireland		
Democratic Left	Democratic Left	
Labour Party	Labour Party (Irish: Páirtí an Lucht Oibre)	Labour
Portugal		
Democratic Unity Coalition	Coligação Democrática Unitária	CDU
Portuguese Communist Party	Partido Comunista Português	PCP
Ecologist Party "The Greens"	Partido Ecologista "Os Verdes"	PEV
Estonia		
People's Union of Estonia	Eestimaa Rahvaliit	Rahvaliit
Estonian United Left Party	Eestimaa Ühendatud Vasakpartei	
Romania		
Democratic National Salvation Front	Frontul Democrat al Salvării Naţionale	FDSN
Romanian Party of Social Democracy	Partidul Social Democrat Român	PSDR
Socialist Democratic Party of Romania	Partidul Social Democrat	PSD
Cooperative Party	Partidul Cooperatist	PC
Republican Party	Partidul Republican	PR

Bibliography

Achen, Christopher H., and Bartels, Larry M. (2004) 'Musical chairs: pocketbook voting and the limits of democratic accountability,' in *Annual Meeting* of the American Political Science Association, Chicago, IL.

Aguilar, Paloma, and Sanchez-Cuena, Ignacio (2008) 'Performance or representation? The determinants of voting in complex political contexts,' in *Controlling Governments: Voters, Institutions, and Accountability*, 105–30. Cambridge: Cambridge University Press.

Alesina, Alberto, and Rosenthal, Howard (1995) *Partisan Politics, Divided Government, and the Economy*. New York: Cambridge University Press.

Althaus, Scott L. (2003) *Collective Preferences in Democratic Politics: Opinion Surveys and the Will of the People*, New York: Cambridge University Press.

Alvarez, R. Michael, and Brehm, John (2002) *Hard Choices, Easy Answers: Values, Information, and American Public Opinion*, Princeton: Princeton University Press.

Alvarez, R. Michael, and Nagler, Jonathan (1998) 'When politics and models collide: estimating models of multiparty elections,' *American Journal of Political Science* 42, no. 1: 55–96.

Andersen, Robert, and Evans, Geoffrey (2003) 'Who Blairs wins? Leadership and voting in the 2001 election,' *British Elections and Parties Review* 13, no. 1: 229–47.

Andersen, Robert, Tilley, James, and Heath, Anthony F. (2005) 'Political knowledge and enlightened preferences: party choice through the electoral cycle,' *British Journal of Political Science* 35, no. 2: 285–302.

Anderson, Christopher J. (2000) 'Economic voting and political context: a comparative perspective,' *Electoral Studies* 19, no. 2–3 151–70.

— 'The dynamics of public support for coalition governments,' *Comparative Political Studies* 28, no. 3 (1995): 350–83.

Anderson, Christopher J., and Beramendi, Pablo (2012) 'Left parties, poor voters, and electoral participation in advanced industrial societies,' *Comparative Political Studies* 45, no. 6: 714–46.

Anderson, Christopher J, and Brettschneider, F. (2003) "The Likable Winner versus the Competent Loser: Candidate Images and the German Election of 2002." *German Politics and Society* 21, no. 1: 95–118.

Anderson, Christopher J., and Hecht, Jason D. (2012) 'Voting when the economy goes bad, everyone is in charge, and no one is to blame: the case of the 2009 German election,' *Electoral Studies* 31, no. 1: 5–19.

Arceneaux, Kevin (2008) 'Can partisan cues diminish democratic accountability?' *Political Behavior* 30, no. 2: 139–60.

Arian, Asher, and Shamir, Michal (2001) 'Candidates, parties and blocs,' *Party Politics* 7, no. 6: 689–710.

Bækgaard, Martin, and Jensen, Carsten (2012) 'The dynamics of competitor party behaviour,' *Political Studies* 60, no. 1: 131–46.

Baldassarri, Delia (2013) *The Simple Art of Voting: The cognitive shortcuts of Italian voters*, New York: Oxford University Press.

Baldini, Gianfranco (2011) 'The different trajectories of Italian electoral reforms,' *West European Politics* 34, no. 3: 644–63.

Bargh, John A (1999) 'The cognitive monster: the case against the controllability of automatic stereotype effects,' in *Dual-Process Theories in Social Psychology*, edited by S. Chaiken and Y. Trope, 361–82. New York: Guilford Press.

Barnea, Shlomit, and Rahat, Gideo (2011) 'Out with the old, in with the "new": what constitutes a new party?' *Party Politics* 17, no. 3: 303–20.

Barnes, Samuel H., Peter McDonough, and Antonio Lopez Pina (1985) 'The development of partisanship in new democracies: the case of Spain,' *American Journal of Political Science* 29, no. 4: 695–720.

Bartels, Larry M. (1996) "Uninformed Votes: Information Effects in Presidential Elections." *American Journal of Political Science* 40, no. 1: 194–230.

Bartolini, Stefano, and Mair, Peter (1990) *Identity, Competition, and Electoral Availability: The stabilization of European electorates 1885-1985*, New York: Cambridge University Press.

Basinger, Scott J., and Lavine, Howard (2005) 'Ambivalence, information, and electoral choice,' *American Political Science Review* 99, no. 2: 169–84.

Bean, Clive, and Mughan, Anthony (1989) 'Leadership effects in parliamentary elections in Australia and Britain,' *American Political Science Review* 83, no. 4: 1165–79.

Bengtsson, Asa (2004) 'Economic voting: the effect of political context, volatility and turnout on voters' assignment of responsibility,' *European Journal of Political Research* 43, no. 5: 749–67.

Bennett, Stephen Earl (1989) 'Trends in Americans' political information, 1967-1987,' *American Politics Research* 17, no. 4: 422–35.

Berggren, Heidi M. (2000) 'Institutional context and reduction of the resource bias in political sophistication,' *Political Research Quarterly* 54, no. 3: 531–52.

Bernhardt, M. Daniel, and Ingberman, Daniel E. (1985) 'Candidate reputations and the "incumbency Effect",' *Journal of Public Economics* 27, no. 1: 47–67.

Bielasiak, Jack (1997) 'Substance and process in the development of party systems in East Central Europe,' *Communist and Post-Communist Studies* 30, no. 1: 23–44.

— 'The institutionalization of electoral and party systems in postcommunist states,' *Comparative Politics* 34, no. 2 (2002): 189–210.

Birch, Sarah. (1998) "Party System Formation and Voting Behavior in the Ukrainian Parliamentary Elections of 1994." In *Contemporary Ukraine: Dynamics of Post-Soviet Transformation*, edited by Taras Kuzio, 139–160. Armonk, NY: ME Sharpe.

— 'Electoral systems and party system stability in Post-Communist Europe,' In *The Annual Meeting of the American Political Science Association*, San Francisco, CA, 2001.

Brady, Henry E., and Sniderman, Paul M. (1985) 'Attitude attribution: a group basis for political reasoning,' *The American Political Science Review* 79, no. 4: 1061–78.

Cain, Bruce E., Ferejohn, John A., and Fiorina, Morris (1987) *The Personal Vote: Constituency service and electoral independence*, Cambridge, Mass.: Harvard University Press.

Carmines, Edward G., and Nicholas J. D'amico (2015) 'Heuristic decision-making,' *Emerging Trends in the Social and Behavioral Sciences: An interdisciplinary, searchable, and linkable resource*. doi: 10.1002/9781118900772.etrds0159

Chaiken, Shelly (1980) 'Heuristic versus systematic information processing and the use of source versus message cues in persuasion,' *Journal of Personality and Social Psychology* 39, no. 5: 752–766.

Chen, Serena, and Chaiken, Shelly (1999) 'The heuristic-systematic model in its broader context,' in *Dual-Process Theories in Social Psychology*, edited by S. Chaiken and Y. Trope, 73–96. New York: Guilford Press.

Cho, Sungdai, and Endersby, James W. (2003) "Issues, the Spatial Theory of Voting, and British General Elections: A Comparison of Proximity and Directional Models." *Public Choice* 114, no. 3–4: 275–293.

Clarke, Harold D (2009) *Performance Politics and the British Voter*, New York: Cambridge University Press.

Conover, Pamela Johnston, and Feldman, Stanley (1989) 'Candidate perception in an ambiguous world: campaigns, cues, and inference processes,' *American Journal of Political Science* 33, no. 4: 912–40.

Converse, Philip E (1964) 'The nature of belief systems in mass publics,' in *Ideology and Discontent*, edited by David E. Apter, 206–61. New York: The Free Press.

Coppedge, M. (1998) "The Dynamic Diversity of Latin American Party Systems." *Party Politics* 4, no. 4: 547–568.

Curtice, John, and Hunjan, Sarinder (2006) 'The impact of leadership evaluations on voting behaviour: do the rules matter?' *Centre for Research into Elections and Social Trends (CREST) Working Paper*, no. 110.

Dalton, Russell J., and McAllister, Ian (2015) "Random Walk or Planned Excursion? Continuity and Change in the Left–Right Positions of Political Parties." *Comparative Political Studies* 48, no. 6: 759–87.

Dancey, Logan, and Sheagley, Geoffrey (2013) 'Heuristics behaving badly: party cues and voter knowledge,' *American Journal of Political Science* 57, no. 2: 312–25.

De Vries, Catherine E., and Giger, Nathalie (2014) 'Holding governments accountable? Individual heterogeneity in performance voting,' *European Journal of Political Research* 53, no. 2: 345–62.

Dix, Robert H. (1992) 'Democratization and the institutionalization of Latin American political parties,' *Comparative Political Studies* 24, no. 4: 488–511.

Downs, Anthony (1957) *An Economic Theory of Democracy*, New York: Harper.

Duch, Raymond M., and Stevenson, Randy (2008) *The Economic Vote: How political and economic institutions condition election results*, New York: Cambridge University Press.

Eagly, Alice H., and Chaiken, Shelly (1993) *The Psychology of Attitudes*, Orlando, FL, US: Harcourt Brace Jovanovich College Publishers.

Ensley, Michael J. (2007) 'Candidate divergence, ideology, and vote choice in U.S. Senate Elections,' *American Politics Research* 35, no. 1: 103–22.

Ersson, Svante, and Lane, Jan Erik (1998) 'Electoral instability and party system change in Western Europe,' in *Comparing Party System Change*, edited by Paul Pennings and Jan-Erik Lane, 23–39. New York: Routledge.

Evans, Geoffrey, and Andersen, Robert. (2005) "The Impact of Party Leaders: How Blair Lost Labour Votes." *Parliamentary Affairs* 58, no. 4: 818–836.

Evans, Jocelyn A. J. (2002) "In Defence of Sartori." *Party Politics* 8, no. 2: 155–174.

Ezrow, Lawrence (2010) *Linking Citizens and Parties: How electoral systems matter for political representation*, Oxford: Oxford University Press.

Farrell, Joseph (1995) 'Berlusconi and Forza Italia: new force for old?' *Modern Italy* 1, no. 1: 40–52.

Fiorina, Morris (1981) *Retrospective Voting in American National Elections*, New Haven, CT: Yale University Press.

Flanagan, Scott C., and Dalton, Russell J. (1984) 'Parties under stress: realignment and dealignment in advanced industrial societies,' *West European Politics* 7, no. 1: 7–23.

Fortunato, David, and Stevenson, Randolph T. (2013) 'Perceptions of partisan ideologies: the effect of coalition participation,' *American Journal of Political Science* 57, no. 2: 459–77.

Fraile, Marta (2014) 'Do information-rich contexts reduce knowledge inequalities? The contextual determinants of political knowledge in Europe,' *Acta Politica* 48, no. 2: 119–43.

Franklin, Mark N. (2004) *Voter Turnout and the Dynamics of Electoral Competition in Established Democracies since 1945*, New York: Cambridge University Press.

Friedrich, Carl J. *Trends of Federalism in Theory and Practice*. Praeger, 1968.

Garzia, Diego (2013) 'The rise of party/leader identification in Western Europe,' *Political Research Quarterly* 66, no. 3: 533–44.

Giner-Sorolla, Roger (1999) 'Affect in attitude,' *Dual Process Theories in Social Psychology*, 441–61.

Golder, Matt, and Stramski, Jacek (2010) 'Ideological congruence and electoral institutions,' *American Journal of Political Science* 54, no. 1: 90–106.

Gomez, Brad T., and J. Wilson, Matthew (2001) 'Political sophistication and economic voting in the American electorate: a theory of heterogeneous attribution,' *American Journal of Political Science* 4, no. 5 899–914.

— 'Rethinking symbolic racism: evidence of attribution bias.' *The Journal of Politics* 68, no. 3 (2006): 611–25.

Gordon, Stacy B., and Segura, Gary M. (1997) 'Cross-national variation in the political sophistication of individuals: capability or choice?' *The Journal of Politics* 59, no. 1: 126–47.

Graetz, Brian, and McAllister, Ian (1987) 'Party leaders and election outcomes in Britain, 1974–1983,' *Comparative Political Studies* 19, no. 4: 484–507.

Gronke, Paul (2000) 'The electorate, the campaign, and the office,' Ann Arbor: University of Michigan Press.

Grönlund, Kimmo, and Milner, Henry (2006) 'The determinants of political knowledge in comparative perspective,' *Scandinavian Political Studies* 29, no. 4 386–406.

Grotz, Florian, and Weber, Till (2015) 'New parties, information uncertainty, and government formation: evidence from Central and Eastern Europe,' *European Political Science Review* FirstView: 1–24.

Harmel, Robert, and Janda, Kenneth (1994) 'An integrated theory of party goals and party change,' *Journal of Theoretical Politics* 6, no. 3: 259–87.

Harmel, Robert, and Robertson, John D. (1985) "Formation and Success of New Parties A Cross-National Analysis." *International Political Science Review* 6, no. 4: 501–23.

Haughton, Tim (2004) 'Explaining the limited success of the Communist-successor left in Slovakia: the case of the party of the democratic left (SDL)' *Party Politics* 10, no. 2: 177–91.

Healy, Andrew, and Malhotra, Neil (2013) 'Retrospective voting reconsidered,' *Annual Review of Political Science* 16, no. 1: 285–306.

Hellmann, Olli. (2011) *Political Parties and Electoral Strategy: The development of party organization in East Asia.* Basingstoke: Palgrave Macmillan.

Hellwig, Timothy (2001) 'Interdependence, government constraints, and economic voting,' *Journal of Politics* 63, no. 4: 1141–62.

— "Constructing Accountability Party Position Taking and Economic Voting." *Comparative Political Studies* 45, no. 1 (2012): 91–118.

Hellwig, Timothy, and Marinova, Dani M. (2015) 'More misinformed than myopic: economic retrospections and the voter's time horizon,' *Political Behavior* 37, no. 4: 865–87.

Hellwig, Timothy, and Samuels, David (2008) 'Electoral accountability and the variety of democratic regimes,' *British Journal of Political Science* 38, no. 1: 65–90.

Hinich, Melvin J., and Munger, Michael C. (1997) *Analytical Politics*, New York: Cambridge University Press.

Hooghe, Marc (2004) 'Political socialization and the future of politics,' *Acta Politica* 39, no. 4: 331–41.

Hopkin, Johnathan, and Paolucci, Caterina (1999) 'The business firm model of party organisation: cases from Spain and Italy,' *European Journal of Political Research* 35, no. 3: 307–39.

Huber, John D., and Powell, G. Bingham (1994) 'Congruence between citizens and policymakers in two visions of liberal democracy,' *World Politics* 46, no. 2: 291–326.

Huckfeldt, Robert R., and Sprague, John (1995) *Citizens, Politics and Social Communication: Information and influence in an election campaign*, New York: Cambridge University Press.

Ingberman, Daniel E. (1985) 'Running against the status quo: institutions for direct democracy referenda and allocations over time,' *Public Choice* 46, no. 1: 19–43.

Inglehart, Ronald (1977) *The Silent Revolution: Changing values and political styles among Western publics*, Princeton, N.J.: Princeton University Press.

Jackman, Simon, and Sniderman, Paul M. (2002) 'Institutional conception of choice spaces: a political conception of political psychology,' in *Political Psychology*, edited by Kristen Renwick Monroe, 209–24. Mahwah, NJ: Lawrence Erlbaum Associates.

Janda, Kenneth (1980) *Political Parties: A cross-national survey*, New York: Free Press.

Jennings, M. Kent (1987) 'Residues of a movement: the aging of the American protest generation,' *American Political Science Review* 81, no 2: 367–82.

Jungerstam-Mulders, Susanne (2006) 'Party system change in post-communist EU member states,' in *Post-Communist EU Member States: Parties and party systems*, edited by Susanne Jungerstam-Mulders, 233–50, Aldershot: Ashgate.

Kaase, M. (1994) 'Is there personalization in politics? Candidates and voting behavior in Germany,' *International Political Science Review* 15, no. 3: 211–30.

Kahn, Kim Fridkin, and Kenney, Patrick J. (1997) 'A model of candidate evaluations in senate elections: the impact of campaign intensity,' *The Journal of Politics* 59, no. 4: 1173–1205.

Karvonen, Lauri (2010) *The Personalisation of Politics: A study of parliamentary democracies*, Colchester: ECPR Press.

Katz, Richard S., and Koole, Ruud, eds. (1999) "Special Issue: Political Data Yearbook." *European Journal of Political Research* 36, no. 3–4: 317–547.

Kayser, Mark, and Peress, Michael (2012) "Benchmarking across Borders: Electoral Accountability and the Necessity of Comparison." *American Political Science Review* 106, no. 3: 661–684.

Kedar, Orit (2009) *Voting for Policy, Not Parties: How voters compensate for power sharing*, New York: Cambridge University Press.

Key, V. O. (1966) *The Responsible Electorate: Rationality in presidential voting, 1936-1960.* Belknap Press of Harvard University Press.

Klingemann, Hans-Dieter, and Wessels, Bernhard (2009) 'How voters cope with the complexity of their political environment: differentiation of political supply, effectiveness of electoral institutions, and the calculus of voting,' in *The Comparative Study of Electoral Systems*, edited by Hans-Dieter Klingemann, 237–65. New York: Oxford University Press.

Knutsen, Oddbjørn, and Kumlin, Staffan (2005) 'Value orientations and party choice,' in *The European Voter: A comparative study of modern democracies*, edited by Jacques Thomassen, 125–67. New York: Oxford University Press.

Koch, Jeffrey W. (2003) 'Being certain versus being right: citizen certainty and accuracy of house candidates' ideological orientations,' *Political Behavior* 25, no. 3: 221–46.

— 'Electoral competitiveness and the voting decision evidence from the pooled senate election study,' *Political Behavior* 20, no. 4 (1998): 295–311.

Korasteleva, Elena A. (2000) 'Electoral volatility in post-communist Belarus,' *Party Politics* 6, no. 3: 343–58.

Kreuzer, Marcus, and Pettai, Vello (2003) 'Patterns of political instability: affiliation patterns of politicians and voters in post-communist Estonia, Latvia, and Lithuania,' *Studies in Comparative International Development* 38, no. 2; 76–98.

Lachat, Romain (2008) 'The impact of party polarization on ideological voting,' *Electoral Studies* 27, no. 4: 687–98.

Lane, Jan-Erik (2008) *Comparative Politics: The principal-agent perspective*, London, New York: Routledge.

Langley, Patrick W., Herbert A. Simon, Gary F. Bradshaw, and Jan M. Zytkow (1987) *Scientific Discover: An account of the creative processes*, Boston, MA: MIT Press.

Langton, Kenneth P. (1984): 'Persistence and change in political confidence over the life-span: embedding life-cycle socialization in context,' *British Journal of Political Science* 14, no. 4: 461–81.

Lau, Richard R. (2003)"Models of Decision-Making." In *Oxford Handbook of Political Psychology*, edited by David O. Sears, Leonie Huddy, and Robert Jervis, 19–59. New York, NY: Oxford University Press.

Lau, Richard R., and Redlawsk, David P. (2001) 'Advantages and disadvantages of cognitive heuristics in political decision-making,' *American Journal of Political Science* 45, no. 4: 951–71.

— *How Voters Decide: Information processing in election campaigns*, New York: Cambridge University Press, 2006.

Laver, Michael. (1989) "Party Competition and Party System Change." *Journal of Theoretical Politics* 1, no. 3: 301–324.

Lavine, Howard, and Gschwend, Thomas (2007) 'Issues, party and character: the moderating role of ideological thinking on candidate evaluation,' *British Journal of Political Science* 37, no. 1: 139–63.

Leeson, Peter T. (2008) 'Media freedom, political knowledge, and participation,' *The Journal of Economic Perspectives* 22, no. 2:.

Lenz, Gabriel. (2011) "Understanding and Curing Myopic Voting." *Unpublished Paper, Massachusetts Institute of Technology.*

— (2013) *Follow the Leader?: How voters respond to politicians' policies and performance*: Chicago: University of Chicago Press.

Lewis-Beck, Michael S. (1988) *Economics and Elections: The major Western democracies*, Ann Arbor: University of Michigan Press.

Lewis-Beck, Michael S., and Mitchell, Glenn E. (1993) 'French electoral theory: the national front test,' *Electoral Studies* 12, no. 2: 112–27.

Lewis-Beck, Michael S., and Stegmaier, Mary (2013) 'The VP-Function revisited: a survey of the literature on vote and popularity functions after over 40 years,' *Public Choice* 157, no. 3–4: 367–85.

Lijphart, Arend. (1984) "Measures of Cabinet Durability: A Conceptual and Empirical Evaluation." *Comparative Political Studies* 17, no. 2: 265–79.

Lijphart, Arend, and Aitkin, Don (1994) *Electoral Systems and Party Systems: A study of twenty-seven democracies, 1945-1990*, Oxford; New York: Oxford University Press.

Lippman, Walter. (1925) *The Phantom Public*, New York: Harcourt, Brace.

Lodge, Milton, and Taber, Charles S. (2000) 'Three steps toward a theory of motivated political reasoning,' in *Elements of Reason: Cognition, choice, and the bounds of rationality*, edited by Arthur Lupia, Mathew D. McCubbins, and Samuel L. Popkin, 183–213. New York: Cambridge University Press.

Lupia, Arthur, and McCubbins, Mathew D. (1998) *The Democratic Dilemma: Can citizens learn what they need to know?* New York: Cambridge University Press.

Luskin, Robert C. (1987) 'Measuring political sophistication,' *American Journal of Political Science* 31, no.4: 856–99.

Maddens, Bart, and Hajnal, Istvan (2001) 'Alternative models of issue voting: the case of the 1991 and 1995 elections in Belgium,' *European Journal of Political Research* 39, no. 3: 319–46.

Maguire, Maria (1983) 'Is there still persistence? Electoral change in Western Europe, 1948–1979,' in *Western European Party Systems: Continuity and change*, edited by Hans Daalder and Peter Mair, 67–94. London: Sage.

Maheswaran, Durairaj, and Chaiken, Shelly (1991) 'Promoting systematic processing in low-motivation settings: effect of incongruent information on processing and judgment,' *Journal of Personality and Social Psychology* 61, no. 1: 13.

Mainwaring, Scott (1998) 'Party systems in the third wave,' *Journal of Democracy* 9, no. 3: 67–81.

Mainwaring, Scott, and Torcal, Mariano (2006) 'Party system institutionalization and party system theory after the third wave of democratization,' In *Handbook of Political Parties*, edited by Richard S. Katz and William Crotty, 204–27. London: Sage.

Mainwaring, Scott, and Edurne Zoco (2007) 'Political sequences and the stabilization of interparty competition: electoral volatility and new democracies,' *Party Politics* 13, no. 2 :155–78.

Mair, Peter (1997) *Party System Change: Approaches and interpretations*, Oxford: Oxford University Press.

Mair, Peter, Muller, Wolfgang, and Plasser, Fritz (2004) *Political Parties and Electoral Change: Party responses to electoral markets*, London: Sage.

Mancini, Paolo (2013) 'Media fragmentation, party system, and democracy,' *The International Journal of Press/Politics* 18, no. 1 :43–60.

Maravall, José María (2006) 'La democracia y la Supervivencia de Los Gobiernos,' *Revista Española de Ciencia Política* 15, no. 1 :9–45.

Marcus, George E., and MacKuen, Michael B. (1993) 'Anxiety, enthusiasm, and the vote: the emotional underpinnings of learning and involvement during presidential campaigns,' *American Political Science Review* 87, no. 3 :672–85.

Marcus, George E., Neuman, W. Russell, and MacKuen, Michael B. (2000) *Affective Intelligence and Political Judgment*, Chicago: University of Chicago Press.

Marquis, Lionel (2010) 'Understanding political knowledge and its influence on voting preferences in the 2007 Federal Election,' *Swiss Political Science Review* 16, no. 3 :425–56.

McAllister, Ian. "Leaders." In *Comparing Democracies: Elections and Voting in Global Perspective*, edited by Lawrence LeDuc, Richard G. Niemi, and Pippa Norris, 280–298. New York: Sage, 1996.

McDermott, Monika L. (1998) 'Race and gender cues in low-information elections,' *Political Research Quarterly* 51, no. 4 :895–918.

McFadden, Daniel. (1974) "Conditional Logit Analysis of Qualitative Choice Behaviour." In *Frontiers in Econometrics*, edited by P. Zarembka, 105–42. New York: Academic Press.

McGraw, Kathleen M., and Neil Pinney. (1990) "The Effects of General and Domain-Specific Expertise on Political Memory and Judgment." *Social Cognition* 8, no. 1: 9–30.

Meleshevich, Andrey A. (2007) *Party Systems in Post-Soviet Countries: A comparative study of political institutionalization in the Baltic States, Russia, and Ukraine*, New York: Palgrave Macmillan.

Merril, Samuel, and Bernard Grofman. *A Unified Theory of Voting: Directional and proximity spatial models*, New York: Cambridge University Press, 1999.

— "Directional and Proximity Models of Voter Utility and Choice: A New Synthesis and an Illustrative Test of Competing Models." *Journal of Theoretical Politics* 9 no. 1 (1997): 25–48.

Mill, John Stuart. (1958) *Considerations on Representative Government*. Liberal Arts Press.

Millard, F. (2003) "Elections in Poland 2001: Electoral Manipulation and Party Upheaval." *Communist and Post-Communist Studies* 36, no. 1: 69–86.

Mishler, William, and Rose, Richard (2007) 'Generation, age, and time: the dynamics of political learning during Russia's transformation,' *American Journal of Political Science* 51, no. 4 :822–34.

Müller-Rommel, Ferdinand. (2002) "The Lifespan and the Political Performance of Green Parties in Western Europe." *Environmental Politics* 11, no. 1: 1–16.

Mudde, Cas (1996) 'The paradox of the anti-party party insights from the extreme right,' *Party Politics* 2, no. 2 :265–76.

Multiple authors (1960) *The American Voter*, New York: John Wiley and Sons.

Multiple authors (2009) 'Media system, public knowledge and democracy: a comparative study,' *European Journal of Communication* 24, no. 1: 5–26.

Multiple authors (2011) *Political Parties and Democratic Linkage: How Parties Organize Democracy*. New York: Oxford University Press.

Multiple authors (1996) *What Americans Know about Politics and Why It Matters*, New Haven, CT: Yale University Press.

Multiple authors (1998) *Institutional Design in Post-Communist Societies: Rebuilding the ship at sea*, Cambridge, U.K.; New York, NY, USA: Cambridge University Press.

Multiple authors (2014) 'When extremism pays: policy positions, voter certainty, and party support in postcommunist Europe,' *The Journal of Politics* 76, no. 2: 535–47.

Multiple authors (1983) 'The novice and the expert: knowledge-based strategies in political cognition,' *Journal of Experimental Social Psychology* 19, no. 4: 381–400.

Multiple authors (2000) 'Fission and fusion of parties in Estonia, 1987–1999,' *Journal of Baltic Studies* 31, no. 4: 329–57.

Multiple authors (1989) *Induction Processes of Inference, Learning, and Discovery*. Cambridge, Mass.: MIT Press.

Multiple authors (1995) *Essentials of Neural Science and Behavior*. Norwalk, CT: Appleton & Lange.

Multiple authors (1999) 'Convergence and divergence in advanced capitalist democracies,' in *Continuity and Change in Contemporary Capitalism*, edited by Herbert Kitschelt, 427–60. Cambridge, UK; New York, NY: Cambridge University Press.

Multiple authors (1999) *Post-Communist Party Systems: Competition, Representation, and Inter-Party Cooperation*. New York: Cambridge University Press.

Multiple authors (2001) 'The political environment and citizen competence,' *American Journal of Political Science* 45, no. 2: 410–24.

Multiple authors (1995) "Political Sophistication and Models of Issue Voting." *British Journal of Political Science* 25, no. 4: 453–83.

Nadeau, Richard, Blais, André, Nevitte, Neil, and Gidengil, Elisabeth (2000) 'It's unemployment, Stupid! Why perceptions about the job situation hurt the liberals in the 1997 election,' *Canadian Public Policy/Analyse de Politiques* 26, no. 1 :77–93.

Nadeau, Richard, Niemi, Richard G., Fan, D. P., and Amato, T. (1999) 'Elite economic forecasts, economic news, mass economic judgments, and presidential approval,' *The Journal of Politics* 61, no. 1 :109–35.

Nadeau, Richard, Niemi, Richard G., and Yoshinaka, Antoine (2002) 'A cross-national analysis of economic voting: taking account of the political context across time and nations,' *Electoral Studies* 21, no. 3 :403–23.

Norpoth, H. (2002) 'On a short leash term limits and the economic voter,' in *Economic Voting*, edited by Han Dorussen and Michaell Taylor, 121–41. London: Psychology Press.

O'Dwyer, Conor (2004) 'Runaway state building: how political parties shape states in post-communist Eastern Europe,' *World Politics* 56, no. 4 :520–53.

Paldam, Martin. (1991) "How Robust Is the Vote Function? A Study of Seventeen Nations over Four Decades." In *Economics and Politics: The Calculus of Support*, 9–32. Ann Arbor, MI: University of Michigan Press.

Palfrey, Thomas R., and Poole, Keith T. (1987) 'The relationship between information, ideology, and voting behavior,' *American Journal of Political Science* 31, no. 3 :511–30.

Panebianco, Angelo (1988) *Political Parties: Organization and power*, New York: Cambridge University Press.

Pattie, C., and R. Johnston (2001) 'A low turnout landslide: abstention at the British general election of 1997,' *Political Studies* 49, no. 2: 286–305.

Pedersen, Morgens N. (1979) 'The dynamics of European party systems: changing patterns of electoral volatility,' *European Journal of Political Research* 7, no. 1: 1–26.

Petty, Richard E., and Caeioppo, John T. (1986) *The Elaboration Likelihood Model of Persuasion*, Springer.

Pitkin, Hanna Fenichel (1967) *The Concept of Representation*, Berkeley: University of California Press.

Poguntke, Thomas, and Webb, Paul D. (2005) *The Presidentialization of Politics: A comparative study of modern democracies*, Oxford; New York: Oxford University Press.

Popkin, Samuel L. (1991) *The Reasoning Voter: Communication and persuasion in presidential campaigns*, Chicago, IL: University of Chicago Press.

Powell, Eleanor Neff, and Tucker, Joshua A. (2014) "Revisiting Electoral Volatility in Post-Communist Countries: New Data, New Results and New Approaches." *British Journal of Political Science* 44, no. 1: 123–147.

Powell, G. Bingham (2000) *Elections as Instruments of Democracy: Majoritarian and proportional visions*, New Haven, CT: Yale University Press.

—   'Political representation in comparative politics,' *Annual Review of Political Science* 7, no. 1 (2004): 273–96.
—   'The ideological congruence controversy,' *Comparative Political Studies* 42, no. 12 (2009): 1475–97.
Powell, G. Bingham, and Vanberg, Georg S. (2000) 'Election laws, disproportionality and median correspondence: implications for two visions of democracy,' *British Journal of Political Science* 30, no. 3 :383–411.
Powell, G. Bingham, and Whitten, Guy D. (1993) 'A cross-national analysis of economic voting: taking account of the political context,' *American Journal of Political Science* 37, no. 2 :391–414.
Protsyk, Oleh, and Wilson, Andrew (2003) 'Centre politics in Russia and Ukraine patronage, power and virtuality,' *Party Politics* 9, no. 6 :703–27.
Quinn, Kevin M., Martin, Andrew D., and Whitford, Andrew B. (1999) 'Voter choice in multi-party democracies: a test of competing theories and models,' *American Journal of Political Science* 43, no. 4 :1231.
Rabe-Hesketh, S., and Skrondal, Anders (2008) *Multilevel and Longitudinal Modeling Using Stata*, College Station, Tex.: Stata Press Publication.
Rabinowitz, George, and Macdonald, Stuart Elaine (1989) 'A directional theory of issue voting,' *American Political Science Review* 83, no. 1 :93–121.
Rahat, Gideon, and Sheafer, Tamir (2007) 'The personalization(s) of politics: Israel, 1949–2003,' *Political Communication* 24, no. 1 :65–80.
Rahn, Wendy M. (1993) 'The role of partisan stereotypes in information processing about political candidates,' *American Journal of Political Science* 37, no. 2 :472–96.
Rahn, Wendy M., Aldrich, John H., and Borgida, Eugene (1994) "Individual and Contextual Variations in Political Candidate Appraisal." *American Political Science Review*, 193–199.
Ramonaitė, Ainė (2007) 'Changing nature of partisanship in a post-communist society: comparing 'old' and 'new' parties in Lithuania,' *Lithuanian Political Science Yearbook* :91–110.
Rattinger, Hans, and Kramer, Jurgen (1998) 'Economic conditions and voting preferences in East and West Germany: 1989–1994,' in *Stability and Change in German Elections: How electorates merge, converge, or collide*, edited by Christopher J. Anderson and Carsten Zelle, 99–120. Westport, CT: Greenwood Publishing Group.
Raudenbush, Stephen W., and Bryk, Anthony S. (2002) *Hierarchical Linear Models: Applications and data analysis methods*, Sage.
Redlawsk, David P. (2001) 'You must remember this: a test of the on-line model of voting,' *The Journal of Politics* 63, no. 1 :29–58.
Redlawsk, David P., and Lau, Richard R. (2013) 'Behavioral decision-making,' in *The Oxford Handbook of Political Psychology*, edited by Leonie Huddy, David O. Sears, and Jack S. Levi, 130–64. Oxford; New York: Oxford University Press.

Remmer, Karen L. (1991) 'The political impact of economic crisis in Latin America in the 1980s' *American Political Science Review* 85, no. 3 :777–800.

Robbins, Joseph W., and Hunter, Lance Y. (2012) 'Impact of electoral volatility and party replacement on voter turnout levels,' *Party Politics* 18, no. 6 :919–939.

Roberts, Andrew. (2008) "Hyperaccountability: Economic Voting in Central and Eastern Europe." *Electoral Studies* 27, no. 3: 533–546.

— *The Quality of Democracy in Eastern Europe: Public preferences and policy reforms*, New York: Cambridge University Press, 2009.

Rohrschneider, Robert, and Whitefield, Stephen (2010) 'Consistent choice sets? The stances of political parties towards European integration in ten Central East European democracies, 2003–2007,' *Journal of European Public Policy* 17, no. 1 :55–75.

— *The Strain of Representation: How parties represent diverse voters in Western and Eastern Europe*, Oxford: Oxford University Press, 2012.

— 'Understanding cleavages in party systems: issue position and issue salience in 13 Post-Communist Democracies,' *Comparative Political Studies* 42, no. 2 (2009): 280–313.

Rose, Richard, and Mishler, William (2010) "A Supply-Demand Model of Party-System Institutionalization: The Russian Case." *Party Politics* 16, no. 6: 801–21.

Rose, Richard, and Munro, Neil (2009) *Parties and Elections in New European Democracies*, Colchester: ECPR Press.

Rose, Richard, and Urwin, Derek W. (1970) "Persistence and Change in Western Party Systems Since 1945." *Political Studies* 18, no. 3: 287–319.

Rudolph, T. J. (2003) 'Who's responsible for the economy? The formation and consequences of responsibility attributions,' *American Journal of Political Science* 47, no. 4 :698–713.

Rybář, Marek, and Deegan-Krause, Kevin (2008) 'Slovakia's communist successor parties in comparative perspective,' *Communist and Post-Communist Studies* 41, no. 4 :497–519.

Rydgren, Jens (2005) 'Is extreme right-wing populism contagious? Explaining the emergence of a new party family,' *European Journal of Political Research* 44, no. 3 :413–37.

Samuels, David, and Hellwig, Timothy (2010) 'Elections and accountability for the economy: a conceptual and empirical reassessment'. *Journal of Elections, Public Opinion and Parties* 20, no. 4: 393–419.

Sanchez-Cuenca, Ignacio (2008) 'How can governments be accountable if voters vote ideologically,' in *Controlling Governments: Voters, institutions, and accountability*, 45–81. Cambridge: Cambridge University Press.

Sanders, D., and Gavin, N. (2004) 'Television news, economic perceptions and political preferences in Britain, 1997–2001,' *Journal of Politics* 66, no. 4 :1245–66.

Schaffner, Brian F., and Streb, Matthew J. (2002) 'The partisan heuristic in low-information elections,' *Public Opinion Quarterly* 66, no. 4 :559–81.

Schoonvelde, Martijn (2014) 'Media freedom and the institutional underpinnings of political knowledge,' *Political Science Research and Methods* 2, no. 2 :163–78.

Shabad, Goldie, and Slomezynski, Kazimierz M. (2004) "Inter-Party Mobility among Parliamentary Candidates in Post-Communist East Central Europe." *Party Politics* 10, no. 2: 151–176.

Sharp, Carol, and Lodge, Milton (1985) "Partisan and Ideological Belief Systems: Do They Differ?" *Political Behavior* 7, no. 2: 147–66.

Sikk, Allan (2005) 'How unstable? Volatility and the genuinely new parties in Eastern Europe,' *European Journal of Political Research* 44, no. 3 :391–412.

— 'Newness as a winning formula for new political parties,' *Party Politics* 18, no. 4 (2012): 465–86.

Singer, Matthew M. (2013) 'The global economic crisis and domestic political agendas,' *Electoral Studies* 32, no. 3 :404–10.

Singh, Shane P., and Roy, Jason (2014) 'Political knowledge, the decision calculus, and proximity voting,' *Electoral Studies* 34, no. 1 :89–99.

Smith, Gordon (1989) 'A system perspective on party system change,' *Journal of Theoretical Politics* 1, no. 3 :349–63.

Sniderman, Paul M. (2000) 'Taking sides: a fixed choice theory of political reasoning,' in *Elements of Reason: Cognition, choice, and the bounds of rationality*, edited by Arthur Lupia, Mathew D. McCubbins, and Samuel L. Popkin, 67–84. Cambridge; New York: Cambridge University Press.

Sniderman, Paul M., Brody, Richard A., and Tetlock, Philip (1993) *Reasoning and Choice: Explorations in political psychology*, Cambridge; New York, USA: Cambridge University Press.

Sniderman, Paul M., and Bullock, John (2004) 'A consistent theory of public opinion and political choice: the hypothesis of menu dependence,' in *Studies in Public Opinion: Attitudes, nonattitudes, measurement error, and change*, edited by Willem E. Saris and Paul M. Sniderman, 337–57. Princeton, NJ: Princeton University Press.

Sniderman, Paul M., Glazer, James, and Griffin, Robert (1990) *Information and Democratic Processes*, Urbana: University of Illinois Press.

Somer-Topcu, Z. (2009) "Timely Decisions: The Effects of Past National Elections on Party Policy Change." *The Journal of Politics* 71, no. 1: 238–248.

Spirova, Maria (2007) *Political Parties in Post-Communist Societies: Formation, persistence, and change*, New York: Palgrave Macmillan.

Stefanova, Boyka (2008) 'The 2007 European elections in Bulgaria and Romania,' *Electoral Studies* 27, no. 3 :566–71.

Stoychev, Stoycho P. (2008) 'Europeanization of the Bulgarian party system: dynamics and effects,' *CEU Political Science Journal* 3, no. 1 :2–24.

Szczerbiak, A. (2002) 'Poland's unexpected political earthquake: the September 2001 parliamentary election,' *Journal of Communist Studies and Transition Politics* 18, no. 3 :41–76.

Szczerbiak, Aleks (2004) 'The Polish centre-right's (last?) best hope: the rise and fall of solidarity electoral action,' *Journal of Communist Studies and Transition Politics* 20, no. 3 :55–79.

Taagepera, R., and Grofman, B. (2003) "Mapping the Indices of Seats–votes Disproportionality and Inter-Election Volatility." *Party Politics* 9, no. 6: 659–677.

Tavits, Margit (2006) "Party System Change Testing a Model of New Party Entry." *Party Politics* 12, no. 1: 99–119.

— 'Clarity of responsibility and corruption,' *American Journal of Political Science* 51, no. 1 (2007): 218–29.

— 'On the linkage between electoral volatility and party system instability in Central and Eastern Europe,' *European Journal of Political Research* 47, no. 5 (2008): 537–55.

— "Party Systems in the Making: The Emergence and Success of New Parties in New Democracies." *British Journal of Political Science* 38, no. 1 (2008): 113–33.

— *Post-Communist Democracies and Party Organization*, Cambridge University Press, 2013.

Tocqueville, Alexis (1945) *Democracy in America*, Doubleday,.

Tóka, Gabor. (1997) "Political Parties and Democratic Consolidation in East Central Europe." In *Studies in Public Policy Number 279*. Glasgow, Scotland: Centre for the Study of Public Policy, University of Strathclyde.

Toole, James. (2000) "Government Formation and Party System Stabilization in East Central Europe." *Party Politics* 6, no. 4: 441–61.

Tverdova, Yuliya V. (2011) 'Follow the party or follow the leader? Candidate evaluations, party evaluations, and macropolitical context,' in *Citizens, Context, and Choice: How context shapes citizens' electoral choices*, edited by Russell J. Dalton and Christopher J Anderson, 126–48. New York: Oxford University Press.

Tversky, Amos, and Kahneman, Daniel (1974) 'Judgment under uncertainty: heuristics and biases,' *Science* 185, no. 4157 :1124–31.

Tworzecki, Hubert (2002) *Learning to Choose: Electoral politics in East-Central Europe*, Stanford, Calif.: Stanford University Press.

Van der Brug, Wouter, van der EijK, Cees, and Franklin, Mark (2007) *The Economy and the Vote: Economic conditions and elections in fifteen countries*, New York: Cambridge University Press.

Van der Eijk, Cees, Schmitt, Hermann, and Binder, Tanja (2005) 'Left–right orientations and party choice,' in *The European Voter: A comparative study of modern democracies*, edited by Jacques Thomassen, 166–90. New York: Oxford University Press.

Vowles, Jack, Hellwig, Timothy T., and Coffey, Eva (2009) 'Survey of experts on political parties and globalization: January 2009–April 2009,' Harvard Dataverse Network.

Whitefield, Stephen, and Rohrschneider, Robert (2009) 'Representational consistency: stability and change in political cleavages in Central and Eastern Europe,' *Politics and Policy* 37, no. 4 :667–90.

Whitten, Guy D., and Palmer, Harvey D. (1999) 'Cross-national analyses of economic voting,' *Electoral Studies* 18, no. 1 :49–67.

Zaller, John (1992) *The Nature and Origins of Mass Opinion*, New York: Cambridge University Press.Multiple authors (1960) *The American Voter*, New York: John Wiley and Sons.

Index